And The World Came His Way

Jesse Helms' Contributions To Freedom

By John Dodd

With

David Tyson

Published by:

The Jesse Helms Center
P.O. Box 247
Wingate, N.C. 28174

ISBN: 0-9668679-1-2

Acknowledgements

I would like to acknowledge my wonderful wife Teresa and daughters, Katie and Mary, for their support and love. Many thanks to David Tyson for his writing assistance and Dan Lewis for his excellent research support, without whom this book would not have been possible.   I also must acknowledge the many fine political and federal staff who have served Senator Helms so well over his thirty-year career in the United States Senate.

Dedication

This book is dedicated to all the Special Forces, military advisors and others who bravely fought America's first war against terrorism in Central America during the 1980s.

These men made enormous sacrifices to stop the Libyans, the Iranians, the Iraqis, the Algerians, the PLO, the Soviets and the Cubans from establishing a permanent terrorist base in our hemisphere!

We especially dedicate this book to the memory of those brave young men who did not make it back from America's First War on Terrorism. People like Officer Daniel Scott, who was killed when his helicopter was shot down by terrorists in El Salvador in 1991. And Lieutenant Colonel David J. Pickett and Corporal First Class Ernest Dawson, who were severely wounded in that same attack on an American helicopter. Pickett and Dawson were captured, dragged off and shot in the head by these anti-American terrorists.

Without your sacrifices, Middle Eastern terrorists would have a terrorist base in Central America today — within walking distance of the U.S.-Mexican border.

There were no TV news programs about your heroism, no flag-waving crowds, no movies about your sacrifices.

But we remember you.

And we hope that this nation — which did not understand what you were up against at the time — will one day fully honor the sacrifices and contributions you made to defend our nation, just as we honor the heroics of our men and women who performed so admirably in Afghanistan.

Foreword by Vice President Dick Cheney

One day, Jesse Helms' contributions will belong to history. But for now, he is very busy making history for which we all are extraordinarily grateful. The work of The Jesse Helms Center reflects the spirit of the ideals of the man himself – of his deep commitment to individual liberty, free enterprise, and the cause of democracy and freedom that build good character and a strong nation. Jesse was born in Monroe, not far from the birthplace of Andrew Jackson. Jackson once said that one man with courage makes a majority. Whatever the issue is and whatever the outcome, you can always count on Jesse Helms to be a man of courage, to speak from principle, and to serve the state and the nation. He stood up for North Carolina on the Senate Committee on Agriculture and he stands up for America on the Senate Committee on Foreign Relations. He is a proud member of his political party, but his greater loyalty is to the United States. He has reached across party lines to unite people in support of a strong U.S. foreign policy.

Perhaps Jesse's greatest ideal has been his dedication to serving America. From the day he put on a naval uniform to serve in World War II all the way to this very moment. It's an ideal he wants to pass on. Jesse is a leader who makes a difference for this country every single day. At an event in Washington some years ago, President Ronald Reagan turned to Senator Helms and said, "With your faith, honor and good work it is we who can be thankful to say Jesse Helms is my friend."

Jesse Helms has been a leader in the Senate for three decades, representing North Carolina and the Nation. *And The World Came His Way* is the story of Jesse Helms' leadership for America.

And The World Came His Way

Table of Contents

Introduction 1

I   Helms' Leadership Helps Derail 15
Terrorist State in Nicaragua

II   ¡Mexico Si, Corruption No! 27

III   Presages of Peril 41

IV   Rebuilding America's Defenses 57

V   Chairing Foreign Relations 63

VI   Driving the Flat Tax Bandwagon 81

VII   Seeking a Solution To Social Security 89

VIII Balancing the Budget 105
'Senator No' Says Yes to
Future Generations

IX   Five Elections, Five Victories 111
Helms' Issue-based Campaigns
Transform American Politics

Conclusion 131

Introduction

In 1981, the <u>New York Times</u> described Jesse Helms as "a courtly charmer with the Southern gift of hyperbolic gab. He calls the President's wife 'Miss Nancy' and tells the homeliest page in a Senate elevator that she is the finest beauty in the land. He drags total strangers onto the reserved seats in the Senate subway and invites liberal reporters to lunch in the Senate dining room. Helms has impeccable moral credentials ...."

A 1990 Op-ed piece in the <u>Los Angeles Times</u> further underscored Jesse Helms' reputation for helping others in need: "Helms does believe in charity. Stories of his generosity are legion in North Carolina. Years ago, he adopted a boy with cerebral palsy. His staff uses the full powers of his office to serve and help individual constituents. A vocal Gantt [Harvey Gantt, two-time challenger to Jesse Helms] supporter whose daughter died abroad was amazed when Helms' office helped arrange the official release of the body."

Stories of Jesse Helms' generosity are indeed legion, dating back long before he was elected to public office. But this book will not dwell on the personal contributions Jesse Helms has made to others.

And The World Came His Way focuses on Jesse Helms' incredible role in changing the policies of the country he loves so much.

When Senator Helms announced his retirement, Senator Christopher Dodd (D-CT and a former Chairman of the Democratic National Committee) said it was "the power of his personality that makes him special as a force. People knew if he was the only person on your side, he'd stick with you."

By the time he decided to retire in 2002, after 30 years of service in the Senate, the world had come Jesse Helms' way. He had carried the day on so many issues — from policy in Central America to defense spending to tax policy to welfare spending.

He had transformed American politics — saving Ronald Reagan's career, helping to elect numerous conservative Republicans by building issues for them to run and win on, and by introducing conservatives to cutting-edge political technology.

His vision of a world with more political and economic freedom led him to meet and publicly support people like Margaret Thatcher and Boris Yeltsin, when both were considered taboo by official Washington.

Helms' relationship with world leaders and his knowledge of events in foreign countries produced at least a couple of humorous moments. In 1979, after Margaret Thatcher had become Prime Minister of England, Jimmy Carter's Secretary of State Cyrus Vance said the British were complaining about two Helms' aides who were interfering in negotiations over Rhodesia. Senator Helms responded: "I called Maggie Thatcher. She did not know anything about it." End of discussion.

Long time friends: Margaret Thatcher visits with Senator Helms in his office in the 1970s.

Margaret Thatcher and Mrs. Dorothy Helms help Senator Helms cut the ribbon in 2001, at The Jesse Helms Center.

In November 1972, when Jesse Helms was first elected to the United States Senate, many political observers believed he would simply be a one-term Senator elected by Richard Nixon's landslide over George McGovern. That was the first of many underestimations of Senator Jesse Helms.

During his career, Jesse Helms won five elections, prompting even liberal North Carolina political observers to acknowledge that he was the most powerful and popular politician the state had ever produced.

"By winning five straight U.S. Senate campaigns and serving longer than any other Senator elected by the people in state history, Helms can lay legitimate claim to being North Carolina's most popular politician," said Jack Betts of the Charlotte Observer. (August 22, 2001)

By the mid-1990s, Senator Helms was able to say with a certain degree of satisfaction: "It used to be I had to look around to find somebody to paint the fence. But now — heck, they've got their own paint buckets."

Yes, when Senator Helms announced his retirement, there was unanimity across the political spectrum that he had dramatically changed the direction of the country. Liberals were even forced to acknowledge that Jesse Helms had ushered in a new era in American politics. Steven Hess of the liberal Brookings Institute noted that: "Many of Helms' ideas are not as outstandingly original as they used to be. There are others who are parroting them, and perhaps even some who have gone to the right of Helms. Once that happens, he might start to look like a moderate."

Thirty years after his first election victory, as Jesse Helms prepares to leave the U.S. Senate, other political analysts from across the spectrum are acknowledging the pre-eminent role that he has played in transforming American politics. The <u>Washington Post</u> referred to Jesse Helms "as one of the most powerful conservatives on Capitol Hill for three decades." The <u>New York Times</u> called him "a conservative stalwart for nearly 30 years."

Jesse Helms rose to a position of power in the Senate the old fashioned way: he earned it. Senator Helms put in thousands of hours at home reviewing legislation and briefing reports.

Even his worst critics acknowledge one other fact: he did it all while keeping his integrity intact. There was never even a hint of ethical scandal surrounding him in his 30 years in the Senate.

As a Senator, Jesse Helms delighted in meeting young people interested in learning about their government, and in the past 30 years has met with over 100,000 young people who were visiting Washington, D.C.

In addition, Senator Helms insisted that all of his North Carolina constituents received prompt attention to their problems and requests. His constituent service was considered a model for other Senators to follow — and has been so recognized by numerous publications. The <u>New York Times</u>, not known as a partisan Helms paper, says simply: "Helms' staff is known for giving excellent and impartial constituent services." He was known as a fierce and effective advocate for North Carolina's tobacco farmers and textile workers. He helped owner Jerry Richardson bring the Carolina Panthers NFL football team to Charlotte. Richardson sent Senator Helms a football inscribed with the words "Thank you for helping make my NFL dreams come true."

When Hurricane Fran created enormous damage throughout eastern North Carolina and the Piedmont, Senator Helms made sure North Carolina received sufficient federal aid to rebuild.

Even political publications that are not pro-Helms admit to his strong influence over policy. In November 1983, <u>American Politics</u> wrote:

"Even more than Ronald Reagan, Jesse Helms stands as the symbol of conservatism and the power of the new Right. A patron saint to his followers, Helms is the man liberals love to hate .... There is no doubt that Helms is a force in American politics. His path from a North Carolina radio commentator to Senate gadfly to the 'conscience of conservatism' (in the words of one of the premiere conservative organizations) traces a phenomenal rise in influence and power. As a result of mastering the minutiae of the Senate rules, Helms has been able to exert astonishing control over the legislative agenda."

But Jesse Helms' legacy will not be solely of an effective Senator for his home state of North Carolina.

Senator Jesse Helms will be remembered as a Senator who influenced politics and policies throughout the world. From Washington to Central America to South America, from the former Soviet Union to China to the Middle East, Helms' influence was felt.

His political opponents tried to capitalize on Senator Helms' enormous influence over foreign policy issues, with little success. During the 1984 campaign, Democratic Governor Jim Hunt ran TV ads criticizing Helms' influence on policy in Central America and South America. Helms' longtime media adviser, Earl Ashe, after seeing one Hunt TV ad criticize Helms' foreign policy influence quipped "I don't know if the people understand the details of what Hunt's talking about, but Hunt sure is doing a good job of convincing everyone in North Carolina that their Senator is one of the most powerful men on the planet!"

But Senator Helms and power were an odd combination. Unlike many politicians, Jesse Helms did not seek power for personal aggrandizement. He sought influence to help shape policy. Another odd thing about Helms and power: he often sought influence over issues that were not popular in the polls; he even sought influence over issues that were not in the headlines.

Clarence Thomas Recalls Meeting Jesse Helms

I have been fortunate to know Senator Helms for over 15 years. You know, of course, I was a young upstart when I went to Washington. I heard of the fiery Jesse Helms who was known as Senator "No." It was always interesting. I was a young staffer in '79 [for Missouri Senator John Danforth] and no one knew who I was. I would see Senator Helms in the hall, as I would see other senators, as we traveled from the Russell Senate Office Building to the Capitol. Some senators would never deign to speak to you. In fact, if you got on that little tram going from the Senate Office Building to the Capitol and certain senators got on the tram you had to get off. They only used one seat but you had to get off the whole thing. I did not understand that. If they got on Amtrak, would everybody have to get off Amtrak? But you got off because you were a lowly staffer and you conducted yourself as a lowly staffer. It was different with Senator Helms. When he saw you, he always had a good word. I said to myself, "Oh my goodness he's supposed to be a mean man, why is he always talking? Why does he say good morning? Why does he say good afternoon?" You'd get in the elevator and he would ask you how you're doing or who do you work for. You'd see him talking to little kids and you'd see him talking to other insignificant people like me. I have always been taught that on a personal level you judge a person by the way he or she treats the least among us. I always find it fascinating that people talk in theory about how it's nice to be good to other people but then you see how poorly they treat cafeteria help or janitors or bus drivers — the people who are just doing their jobs and living their lives. I can say that I've only seen Senator Helms treat people with dignity and I think that when we judge him, we should judge him as he treats the least among us. In my experience that has been very well.

Supreme Court Justice Clarence Thomas
and Senator Jesse Helms.

He strongly felt the giveaway of the Panama Canal was a disastrous sign of U.S. weakness that would have catastrophic consequences for the U.S. in Central America. Ultimately, history would prove him right. According to CIA reports, Panama played a key role in shipping Cuban weapons to the communist Sandinistas in Nicaragua, destabilizing the entire region. The issue of the Panama Canal Giveaway is the consummate example of how Jesse Helms the Senator and Jesse Helms the leader of the conservative cause operated in tandem.

Jesse Helms began fighting the giveaway of the Panama Canal back in 1975, during the administration of Gerald Ford. Senator Helms worked privately and publicly to try to persuade the Ford Administration not to give away the Panama Canal. He lost the policy battle with the Ford Administration. It was hell-bent on pursuing the giveaway of the Canal and President Ford had a lot of U.S. Senators on his side.

So Jesse Helms exercised his rights as an American to raise the issue in the next election campaign — the Ford vs. Reagan primary of 1976. Helms and his political operatives made sure Republican voters in the North Carolina primary knew that Gerald Ford was about to give away the Panama Canal. The result: Ronald Reagan won his first primary in North Carolina at a time when his advisors were encouraging him to withdraw from the race. Reagan's career was saved. He fought all the way to the convention in 1976 and all the way to the White House in 1981.

According to the <u>St. Petersburg (FL) Times</u>, "you can make a strong case that without a Helms there could not have been a Reagan .... Had Reagan not revived his collapsing 1976 campaign in North Carolina .... you could argue that Reagan four years later would not have happened."

Even the Democratic <u>Raleigh (N.C.) News & Observer</u>, Helms' most persistent critic, acknowledges:

"Had Reagan not won the Tar Heel presidential primary in 1976, there probably would not have been a Reagan presidency four years later. There seems to be little doubt that U.S. Senator Jesse Helms and his old political organization, The National Congressional Club of Raleigh, turned Reagan's fortunes around .... Reagan's campaign was barely alive. Ford had won all five primaries before North Carolina, and a loss here very well could have ended Reagan's presidential aspirations. GOP leaders were calling for Reagan to head back to his ranch .... Reagan defeated Ford by a 52 percent to 46 percent margin, reviving his campaign and setting the stage for 1980 .... Reagan and his campaign aides, who were attending a campaign dinner in Wisconsin, could hardly believe the news from North Carolina. Not until their plane left for California did they begin to celebrate, [according to Jules Whitecover's book, "Marathon"]. Reagan began throwing a football around with his wife and their son, Ron Jr., while aides drank champagne and marched up and down the aisles singing 'Nothing could be finer than to give Ford a shiner in the primary.' [Their 'victory song' was a takeoff of a North Carolina song 'Nothing could be finer than to be in Carolina.']"

Most political observers acknowledge that Helms effectively used the Panama Canal issue to save Reagan's career in 1976. But the '76 primary was just the beginning of the conservative uprising — there was plenty of life left in the Canal issue. So, Jesse Helms continued to raise the profile of the Panama Canal issue following the '76 primary. The policy side of Helms was angry about the prospect of giving away the Panama Canal and determined to do everything he could to stop it. The political leader in Helms decided that if he could not stop it, he was committed to letting the American people know who voted for it and who voted against it. Then the American people could let their voices be heard in the next election.

In the 1978 elections, 12 of the Senators who voted for the Panama Canal Treaty were defeated, and 4 more retired rather than run again. In the 1980 elections, 9 more Senators who voted for the Panama Canal Treaty were defeated, and another 4 retired. So within four short years, 29 of the Senators who voted to give away the Panama Canal were out of office. And conservatives swept in to take control of the Senate by 1980, helping to usher in the Reagan Revolution. It was largely thanks to Senator Jesse Helms.

After Reagan was inaugurated in 1981, the New York Times took note of Helms' role in bringing to pass the Era of Reagan: "Helms and his political sidekick Thomas F. Ellis, a North Carolina attorney, helped revive Mr. Reagan's flagging 1976 bid for the nomination by orchestrating his upset primary victory in their home state over Gerald Ford. In 1980, Helms campaigned in 22 states for Mr. Reagan and other GOP candidates, and his unique political machine, the Congressional Club of North Carolina, raised an astonishing $4 million nationwide for the Republican standard-bearer."

But Senator Helms was not laying the groundwork for a conservative revolution just in the United States. He was doing his part to help and encourage conservatives around the world. In 1974, a little known conservative member of the British Parliament was refused office space by the State Department because the Labor Party was in power in Great Britain. Senator Helms, a great admirer of this little known conservative from England, offered her working space in his offices when she came to Washington. In time the world would come to know and admire the lady Helms had admired years before. Her name, of course, was Margaret Thatcher. And she would go on to become the strongest ally that Ronald Reagan and conservatives had in fighting to bring down the Iron Curtain.

The players were now in place, now it was time to change some policies.

Senator Helms with the new president (Ronald Reagan), the new senate majority leader (Howard Baker) and the new senator from North Carolina (John East).

I
Helms' Leadership Helps Derail Terrorist State in Nicaragua

Nicaragua is a country less than three hours flight time from the United States. In 1979, Sandinista terrorists — aided by weapons and advice from their terrorist brethren in the Middle East — seized power in Nicaragua. The Sandinistas quickly moved to establish Nicaragua as a base of operations for the world-wide terrorist movement.

Jesse Helms was one of the first to speak out about the threat posed by the terrorist advances in Central America.

Even prior to the election of Ronald Reagan, prior to the debate over "Reagan's aid to the Contras," Jesse Helms was warning about the dangerous situations brewing in Central America. Senator Helms repeatedly took to the floor of the U.S. Senate to denounce Jimmy Carter's Administration for aiding and abetting the Marxist, terrorist revolution in Nicaragua and El Salvador.

Prior to the Sandinista terrorist takeover of Nicaragua, Helms warned of what was to come in a June 21, 1979 Senate speech. Helms said "the truth of the situation is that the Sandinista rebellion is an international operation, financed, trained and supplied from abroad .... We may all realize too late the crucial importance of Nicaragua to the security of the hemisphere."

Helms repeatedly acknowledged the shortcomings of the government of pro-U.S. Nicaragua President Somoza, but he also knew that the alternative movement of the Sandinistas was much worse.

In June and July of 1979, Helms noted that "the Somoza government is neither the best nor the worst of governments in the Western Hemisphere .... his (Somoza's) government *was* authoritarian but not totalitarian. There is no question but that President Somoza was the political boss of his country .... I hold no brief for Somoza, but I do hold a brief for stability, order and freedom."

Helms said we must "be assured that a structure of free government, one that is demonstrably the will of the people, will follow and maintain full political property and human rights."

Senator Helms' point was simple. If you are going to seek the ouster of a pro-U.S. government, at least make sure its replacement will not be worse — and will not threaten the United States.

So while the media was celebrating the onset of the Sandinista revolution, Jesse Helms was warning of its consequences. Senator Helms said on July 17, 1979 that "the resignation of Somoza, deliberately forced by the United States, will come back to haunt the United States for years to come .... Our failure to take bold leadership against the infiltration of the Western Hemisphere means that the eventual price we pay will go higher and higher."

When the Reagan Administration took over from the Carter Administration in January, 1981, the world and particularly the American public was celebrating the release of American hostages from the Iranian terrorists. America thought it was now free from the grip of Middle Eastern terrorists.

Senator Jesse Helms knew better. He knew that terrorists were right in our back yard. When Republicans took over the U.S. Senate in 1981, Helms sought the chairmanship of the Senate Foreign Relations Subcommittee for Western Hemisphere Affairs. Senator Helms told the New York Times in February 1981 why he wanted this position:

> "If we don't start getting things straight with our own hemisphere, starting with Canada, Mexico and all the way south, **our own stability is in jeopardy**."

The Times also noted how hard Helms worked to acquire the most accurate and detailed information on foreign policy matters:

> "Helms is known for having his own pipelines, independent of the other members of the Foreign Relations Committee, to hawkish dissenters at the Defense Department and the CIA who keep him abreast of creeping moderation in the national security establishment. 'Sometimes the committee would meet in executive session for a top-secret briefing,' remembers one person present, 'and you could tell Helms already knew the stuff. It was embarrassing.'"

Helms and his staff had contacts all over Central America (in the Panamanian Defense Force, inside El Salvador's government, in Mexico, in Chile, in Argentina and of course in Nicaragua). Helms' staffers, led by Debora DeMoss, worked overtime to track down every piece of information they could to keep Senator Helms informed. Senator Helms, in turn, used the information to tell America what was at stake in Central America — and yes, to prevent anyone in the Reagan Administration from cutting a deal to let the terrorists off the hook in Central America.

In October 1981, Senator Helms went to the floor of the U.S. Senate and warned of the Middle Eastern terrorists' involvement in Nicaragua:

> "FSLN (Nicaraguan communist movement) cadres are known to have been trained in Lebanon, Libya, and in Algeria under PLO auspices. Arafat himself publicly boasted in Managua, Nicaragua during June 1980 that the FSLN had received training and indeed had fought with the PLO in the Middle East.
>
> A network of terrorist training bases exists today in Nicaragua. Among the locations cited by specialists are Esteli, Montelimar (the former Somoza estate), Somotillo, Ocotal, Tamarindo, Puerto Cabezaz, the Island of Soletiname (in Lake Nicaragua), and several in the Punta Coseguina area (right across from El Salvador) ....

Not only have PLO cadres been active in training camps in Nicaragua, but they have also been reported active in El Salvador and Guatemala. In fact, it has been established that the PLO, Algeria, Libya, and Iraq as well as Cuba, Nicaragua, Mexico and Panama have been supplying weapons and financing to the Salvadoran revolutionary forces ....

There is another aspect to the use of Nicaragua as a safe haven for the Terrorist International. It is known that Nicaragua is issuing false passports to terrorist cadres. Several Cubans using these passports were apprehended in the United States recently. That PLO cadres, as well as other terrorists, could infiltrate the United States, or other countries, using these passports is raising grave concern in a number of capitals ....

In Central America, the vital interests of the United States are directly threatened by the Terrorist International."

Senator Helms' warning about the Nicaraguan passport operation for terrorists was prophetic. In 1993, several of the terrorists who bombed the World Trade Center were found with fake Nicaraguan passports.

The State Department picked up on the theme of terrorist involvement in Nicaragua. A 1985 report by the U.S. State Department entitled "The Sandinistas and Middle Eastern

Radicals" picked up on Helms' warnings about the growing Middle Eastern terrorist threat in Central America.

The report quotes **Libyan** dictator Muammar Qaddafi at a September 1984 rally as saying: "Libyan fighters, arms and backing to the Nicaraguan people have reached them because they fight with us. **They fight America on its own ground**." Qaddafi also threatened to attack "American citizens in their own streets."

Libya's role in establishing a terrorist base in Nicaragua is expounded upon in a separate January 8, 1986 report from the State Department:

"Qaddafi's determination to strike at U.S. interests and to spread his philosophy of revolution has led to a more aggressive Libyan posture in Latin America. Although many governments and groups in this region are wary of Qaddafi, some are willing to accept his financial and military support.

Tripoli views Nicaragua as its base in Central America and accordingly seeks to strengthen the Sandinista dictatorship in Managua.

In addition to several hundred million dollars in economic assistance, Qaddafi's support to the Sandinistas has included anti-aircraft guns, SA-7 surface-to-air missiles and launchers, and small arms. At least several dozen Libyan military personnel are in Nicaragua.

Libyan support has enhanced the Sandinistas' ability to subvert neighboring states."

In addition, "The Sandinistas and Middle Eastern Radicals" report documents a January 23, 1985 meeting including Iranian Prime Minister Mirhussein Musavi where Iranian arms shipments to the Sandinistas and an Iranian-Sandinista oil deal were discussed. According to the State Department, Musavi was "believed to control Iran's terrorist operations."

The Reagan Administration also reported: "As many as 50 Libyan and PLO advisors have been active in Nicaragua. The Libyan advisors have been engaged mostly in servicing the Polish-built MT-2 light helicopters they provided the Nicaraguans. Last May the Libyans also provided the Sandinistas with four small Italian aircraft."

One Sandinista spokesman made no bones about the Sandinistas' alliance with the Middle Eastern Terrorists: "There is a long-standing blood unity between us and the Palestinian revolution. Many of the units belonging to the Sandinista movement were at Palestinian revolution (terrorist) bases in Jordan."

Algeria and Iraq also provided assistance to the anti-American terrorists in El Salvador and Nicaragua.

The State Department's July 1984 "Background Report on the Military Buildup in Nicaragua" documents the role of yet another staunch anti-American terrorist in Nicaragua:

Abu Nidal. Yes, this is the same Abu Nidal who was responsible for the terrorist bombing of the airport in Rome, which resulted in the death of American citizens.

Abu Nidal set up an operation in Central America to recruit terrorists in Mexico City and bring them to Nicaragua. The newly recruited terrorists received phony Nicaraguan passports and terrorist training. Their goal was to bring Middle Eastern terrorism to the United States. Interestingly, nearly nine years later, fake Nicaraguan passports were found on the Middle Eastern terrorists who bombed the World Trade Center the first time — in 1993. At that time, Senator Helms offered an amendment to get tough on the country (Nicaragua) that was harboring this phony passport terrorist operation (a mini-forerunner to the Bush Doctrine which calls for getting tough with countries that host terrorist cells). The Helms Amendment called for the cutoff of all aid to the government of Nicaragua until the government of Nicaragua prosecuted the individuals responsible for providing the terrorists with the fake Nicaraguan passports, and until Nicaragua stopped aiding terrorists. Seventy-seven Senators voted for the Helms Amendment.

There is little question that Jesse Helms was the most powerful spokesman on Capitol Hill for confronting the Middle Eastern and communist-backed terrorist build-up in Central America. "He stood strong with Ronald Reagan when there were huge doubts about a policy of fighting Marxist regimes in Latin America. He was often a lone voice on many issues, but that did not stop him. A lone voice doesn't mean you're wrong," recalled Ken Weinstein of the Hudson Institute.

Indeed Senator Helms found it necessary on several occasions to publicly chastise *Reagan Administration officials* whom he felt were not carrying out the President's policies. In 1982, he warned that Central America was about "to drift into the clutches of Marxist revolutionaries" if stronger action was not taken. In a 1997 profile of Senator Helms, The Weekly Standard noted: "In the 1980s Helms pressured the Reagan Administration to intensify anti-Communist activism in Central America ...." Liberal anti-Helms columnist Jack Germond "blames" Helms for being "the one who forced the State Department into more support for the Contras in Nicaragua."

In August of 2001, Newsweek's Howard Fineman acknowledged Helms' pre-eminent role in stopping the terrorists from taking over Central America. Fineman noted: "It's possible that both Nicaragua and El Salvador would be sort of relic communist regimes were it not for his staunch opposition to them." One can only imagine what would have happened on 9/11 if Middle Eastern terrorists had unfettered use of terrorist bases within three hours flight time of the U.S.

One shudders to think of how many could have died if Middle Eastern terrorists could have moved heavy military equipment from bases in Nicaragua through Mexico and across the porous border into the United States.

And The World Came His Way

These two cartoons illustrate the key role that Senator Jesse Helms played in helping the Reagan Administration defeat the Sandinista terrrorist regime in Nicaragua. Left — Sandinista Leader Daniel Ortga fears Senator Helms becoming chairman of the Senate Foreign Relations Committee. Below — CIA Director William Casey (President Reagan's point man in the Contra War to defeat the Sandinistas) "thanks" Jesse Helms for his support of the administration's policy. Senator Helms was one of a few senators to support Casey's get-tough policy of mining the Nicaragua harbors to prevent Iran, Iraq, Libya, the Soviet Union, Algeria and other terrorist states from shipping weapons into Nicaragua.

History will forever record September 11, 2001 as the day America declared a turning point in America's War on Terrorism. On that day, thousands of Americans were killed in the worst terrorist attack ever on American soil. The World Trade Center towers were left in ruins. The Pentagon was badly damaged.

All because 19 Arab terrorists were able to slip into the United States and hijack four airplanes.

Supported by the courageous leadership of President George W. Bush, Vice-President Dick Cheney and Defense Secretary Donald Rumsfeld, the brave men and women of our armed forces are now dealing a devastating blow to the vast radical Muslim terrorist network that threatens our country.

However, the task of combating anti-American terrorists would have been much more difficult — if not impossible — had the radical Muslim/Middle Eastern terrorist network succeeded in establishing a permanent terrorist base in Nicaragua and El Salvador in the 1980s and early 1990s.

It did not happen.

Because Jesse Helms faced down unholy hell from the media and other liberals — and forced official Washington to confront the terrorist threat in Central America.

And The World Came His Way

II
¡Mexico Si
Corruption No!

"It's very important for Senator Helms, who is one of the most important Senators in the history of the United States and who is the head of the Foreign Relations Committee, to come to Mexico. It is a message of understanding, a message of friendship and a message of a new era of cooperation."

> Eduardo Ibarrola
> Mexico's Deputy Attorney General
> *Charlotte Observer,* April 19, 2000

On June 2, 2000 Vicente Fox was elected President of Mexico, ending the 71-year reign of power and corruption by the ruling Institutional Revolutionary Party (known in Mexico by its Spanish abbreviation PRI).

The 2000 Presidential election was viewed by many international observers as the first honest election in Mexican history. Politicians of all stripes rushed to praise the June 2000 presidential election. President Bill Clinton said: "Mexico's national elections, the freest and fairest in the nation's history, stand as vivid testimony to the depth of the democratic commitment of the Mexican people."

George W. Bush stated: "I think what it indicates is how far reform has come to in Mexico. Obviously there needs to be legal reform in Mexico .... but on political reform, they made great progress."

Even Jimmy Carter was happy. He called the election "a historic turning point of the most profound significance."

For seventy-one years, the left wing Institutional Revolutionary Party (PRI) ruled Mexico with an iron fist. Many Mexicans knew that their government was involved in corruption, the drug trade and rigged elections. But they were powerless to do anything about the corruption of their government. The PRI was simply too strong.

Unfortunately, the Mexicans who were trying to cleanse Mexico's government of the corruption and drug trafficking received little support from political leaders in the United States. Too many political leaders in Washington believed "establishing good relations with Mexico" was more important than establishing fair elections there.

Senator Jesse Helms was one of the few U.S. leaders to publicly challenge the endemic corruption of the Mexican government. In 1986, Senator Helms held a series of four Senate subcommittee hearings on election corruption, fraud and drug trafficking in Mexico. Senator Helms was particularly focused on cleaning up the election process in Mexico.

With the assistance of a source in the Mexican government, Senator Helms produced documents showing that Mexican President Miguel de la Madrid and the PRI had rigged the 1982 Mexican presidential election.

Helms noted that the ruling PRI kept "a double set of books — one public, one private." He called on Mexico's government to open up the election process to international review and inspection.

But Senator Helms did not just make an allegation; he backed it up with hard numbers obtained from internal Mexican sources. The ruling PRI had announced that de la Madrid won the 1982 presidential election with 71.2% of the vote. Helms demonstrated that the ruling party's candidate actually received only 39.8% of the vote.

In August of 1986, after a group of 25 Mexicans complained about Mexican voter fraud, Helms declared that "Mexican citizens are no longer willing to put up with fraud and deceit."

The ruling party in Mexico was incensed by the Helms hearings. They called their Ambassador home for "consultations." They filed a protest with the U.S. State Department. 60,000 Mexican demonstrators protested in Laredo, Texas.

Liberal Democratic Governor Bruce Babbitt complained, "I cannot imagine what has impelled the use of this forum for ungrounded charges of criminal behavior, and for sweeping accusations, on undisclosed evidence of electoral fraud on a scale that bears on the legitimacy of the Mexican government." (Los Angeles Times, July 3, 1986)

De la Madrid himself attacked Senator Helms for holding the hearings saying, "I think in the United States itself they have a well-framed opinion of what Senator Helms is."

Was de la Madrid involved in electoral fraud? De la Madrid's defense of the PRI's voter fraud in the 1986 governor's race in the border state of Chihuahua provided conclusive proof of Senator Helms' claim.

The New York Times provided the following account of de la Madrid's actions in the Chihuahua 1986 governor's race:

"In 1986, however, the PRI decided that the governor's post in the border state of Chihuahua was one it could not lose. PRI operatives brazenly raided polling stations and stuffed fistfuls of pre-marked ballots into the boxes. Mr. Aluarez, then the mayor of the state capital, declared a hunger strike that lasted 40 days.

His protest was widely echoed. Businesses in the state shut down for 48 hours. Voters sat in to block border crossings to the United States. President Miguel de la Madrid defended the "patriotic fraud," saying that the PRI could not allow a strategic border state to fall to the PAN (opposition party)."

Mexico's elections continued to be riddled with fraud throughout the 1980s and 1990s, but the spotlight that Helms shined on the Mexican electoral process began to have a positive effect. Mexico spent more than $1 billion modernizing its electoral system.

More American officials began to speak out.

Prior to the 1994 Mexican presidential election, Secretary of State Warren Christopher publicly warned Mexico's ruling elite about election fraud:

> "To sustain trust in democracy, governments must attack the scourges of corruption and drug trafficking. Government cannot be held accountable if its power can be bought. Authority will not be respected if the rule of law can be defied with impunity."

Senator Helms also helped focus national and world attention on the Mexican government's protection of drug traffickers. In 1989, Senator Helms really stepped up the pressure on Mexican officials who he believed were involved in the drug trade.

> "The problem with the Salinas Administration is not that one or two individuals may have dubious connections, but that a significant number of key officials connected with law enforcement are reported allegedly to be tied to criminals, or

in fact are themselves accused of criminal actions," Helms said in a letter to U.S. Secretary of State James Baker (<u>Washington Post</u>, March 19, 1989).

In March of 1989, Helms publicly alleged that Mexican law enforcement personnel were "protecting drug traffickers."

Leaders of Mexico's ruling elite were outraged. One PRI leader, Hugo Olivares Ventura, called Jesse Helms "an unblushing liar" and contended that Helms' "unfounded accusations stem from his extreme rightist ideology and his interventionist pretensions." (<u>LA Times</u>, March 19, 1989)

Another Mexican official criticized Senator Helms for his "ignorance and total lack of knowledge" about Mexico's efforts to curtail drug trafficking. (<u>Washington Post</u>, March 19, 1989)

That was in March of 1989. The very next month, April 1989, the truth came out.

The April 11, 1989 front-page headline in the <u>Los Angeles Times</u> proclaimed:

<u>POLICE PROTECTED DRUG KINGPIN, MEXICO ADMITS</u>

The <u>LA Times</u> article provided stunning documentation of Senator Helms' claim:

"Mexico's attorney general acknowledged Monday that Miguel Angel Felix Gallardo, one of the world's top cocaine, marijuana and heroin traffickers, ran his multibillion-dollar operation for the last 15 years with the protection of corrupt Mexican police officials.

Attorney General Alvarez del Castillo said that six law enforcement officials, including one of his own men, were detained following the Saturday night arrest of Felix Gallardo in Guadalajara. He said the drug lord fingered the officials.

Alvarez said the officials had supplied Felix Gallardo with weapons and radio equipment, protection for moving drug shipments and information on narcotics investigations."

Eventually, President Salinas' own brother was even sent to prison, "charged with a welter of crimes ranging from drug money laundering to illegal enrichment." (Time, February 1, 1999)

Due to increased American attention, led by Senator Helms, on corruption in the Mexican government, and an increasingly frustrated Mexican public, Mexico's election process gradually improved.

The 1994 presidential election was overseen by 21,000 Mexican officials and over 1,000 foreign observers. The ruling PRI won the presidency again. But in 2000, Mexico finally shed 71 years of corrupt rule by the PRI. President Vicente Fox of the moderate-to-conservative National Action Party (PAN) won the presidency of Mexico. Pandemonium erupted in Mexico City. One observer described it as a "horn-blowing, confetti-throwing, all-night party that spread out from the Angel Independence monument after Fox won." (Toronto Star, July 4, 2000)

President-elect Vicente Fox immediately pledged to tackle the endemic corruption that plagued Mexico:

"We will confront what has become one of the gravest problems of this country which is corruption, impunity and organized crime." (Newsday, July 5, 2000)

Mexicans and Americans can only hope that the Mexican president's war on corruption will be successful.

Certainly Mexicans who spent their lifetime battling the corruption of the PRI deserve the lion's share of the credit for bringing about such a profound change in the Mexican government.

However, the role of Senator Jesse Helms in bringing about change in Mexico cannot be overlooked. He was the one voice in the United States who repeatedly had the courage to stand up and expose the corruption, drug-dealing and election fraud in Mexico. His blunt comments often drew the ire of Mexican government officials, pandering politicians in the United States and editorial writers. But his comments also drew the attention of the media in the United States and throughout the world.

As a result, the U.S. government was forced to confront the issues of Mexican corruption.

In March of 2002, President George W. Bush firmly endorsed the "zero tolerance for corruption" doctrine that Senator Helms had espoused for years. On the eve of a trip to Latin America, President Bush declared:

> "I'm not interested in funding corruption, period. And if a country thinks they're going to get aid from the United States and they're stealing money, they're just not going to get it out of this millennium fund. And hopefully not out of any fund."

Jesse Helms' critics and supporters rarely agree on anything. But they certainly agree that Jesse Helms brings attention to an issue like very few people in public life. And his dogged determination to focus world attention on the corruption in Mexico was vital to breaking the PRI's 71-year reign in that country.

In April 2001, Senator Jesse Helms, Chairman of the Foreign Relations Committee, traveled to Mexico City to hold a series of meetings with President Vicente Fox, Foreign Minister Jorge Castenada, Senator Fernando Margain and other members of the Mexican foreign relations committee.

Senator Helms reassured the Mexican people and its new leadership that, "it is true that over the course of my public life I have criticized certain political leaders of Mexico, and certain government policies those leaders imposed on the Mexican people. But I am not now, and have never been, a critic of Mexico. Mexico and the United States must not merely be good neighbors, we must be partners and friends as well." (<u>Asheville Citizen</u>, April 19, 2001 and the <u>Wall Street Journal</u>, April 19, 2001)

Senator Helms' trip to Mexico City was covered by hordes of reporters who called the meetings "dramatic" and "historic." Helms' colleague, Senator Joe Biden quipped that "I know that no one gives a damn that I'm here. This is all about what Jesse's visit means." (<u>Charlotte Observer</u>, April 19, 2001) What Senator Helms' visit meant was simple: There was a new era dawning in U.S.-Mexican relations.

Senator Helms and the Mexican leadership pledged renewed cooperation in the areas of drug interdiction and immigration. On the topic of immigration, Senator Helms made clear that he was not opposed to Mexicans entering the country; he was just opposed to *illegal* immigration.

Senator Helms noted that: "Whether they came on the Mayflower, or on a 747, almost every U.S. citizen enjoying the privilege of living in our great nation does so because America welcomed them or their parents, their grandparents or their great-grandparents. America owes its prosperity to generations of hard work by legal immigrants. Legal

immigrants built America and America is strengthened by
them today." Senator Helms also singled out immigrants
"from across the Rio Grande."

After the meetings, all sides expressed optimism that a
solution to the immigration problem could be reached

During his visit to Mexico City, Senator Helms also
challenged the new Mexican government to crack down on
drug traffickers in a way that the previous PRI government
had not.

*Senator Helms meets with Mexico's Foreign Secretary Jorge
Castaneda in Mexico City on April 17, 2001.*

"We can't do it alone and neither can you. Our government should offer robust law enforcement advice and assistance," said Senator Helms.

All of the discussions in Mexico City — even on touchy issues like drugs and immigration — were held in a spirit of cooperation.

Toward the end of his visit, Senator Helms declared "we have not come with all the answers to every issue between our two countries. We have come, rather, to try and establish a new spirit of cooperation between our two countries, and to have an honest and open dialogue. We believe there is no end to what we can accomplish if we work together as friends and neighbors." (Charlotte Observer, April 18, 2001)

His gracious Mexican hosts appeared to genuinely appreciate the fact that Senator Helms had come to Mexico. Mexican Senator Fernando Margain said having Jesse Helms lead this mission to Mexico means "more than words" could say. (Wall Street Journal, April 18, 2001) And after the trip, at a White House reception, President Bush "pulled Helms into the Oval Office to thank him for his trip to Mexico. Bush told Helms that Mexican President Fox had called to say that he appreciated the senator's graciousness." (Charlotte Observer, April 29, 2001)

U.S. Senate Foreign Relations Committee Chairman Jesse Helms confers with Fernando Margain, Chairman of the Mexican Senate Foreign Relations Committee in Mexico City on April 18, 2001.

And The World Came His Way

III
Presages of Peril

Jesse Helms was one of the first to speak out about the threat posed by the terrorist advances in Central America. He was right from the beginning about the Communist threat in Central America. And he saved the United States from a dire security threat by keeping terrorists out of America's back yard.

But there were many other major foreign policy issues where Senator Jesse Helms was right from the beginning. Senator Helms warned the world in 1993 that the CIA considered Jean-Bertrand Aristide a "psychopath," a year before Bill Clinton's disastrous decision to send troops into Haiti to restore Aristide. Senator Helms warned the world as early as 1986 about the Panamanian dictator Manuel Noriega, and was criticized by the <u>Washington Post</u> for it. He warned the world in 1988 about Saddam Hussein's acts of violence and terror against his own people. And he has been a consistent critic of Communist China, warning about the threat posed by Beijing in the 1970s and even the 1980s, when many Americans were being wooed by the ping-pong diplomacy of the Chinese.

Jean-Bertrand Aristide

In the 1980s, opposition to "Papa Doc" and "Baby Doc" Duvalier rule in Haiti had been mounting. One of the most outspoken opponents of Duvalier was Jean-Bertrand Aristide. Aristide was a radical priest who believed in "liberation theology," a communist-inspired religious movement in the Third World meant to foment insurrection against pro-Western governments.

Aristide ran for president of Haiti in 1990 at the top of a coalition of leftist parties, and won an overwhelming victory. Seven months later, Aristide was overthrown in a coup and forced to flee the country.

In 1994, with the direct assistance of the Clinton Administration and the U.S. Army, Aristide was returned to power in Haiti, where he remained president for the 16 months left in his term. Aristide then ran for a second presidential term in 2000 and won against little opposition.

Senator Jesse Helms had been a severe critic of the self-described "socialist" Aristide from the start, even before the former priest entered the international spotlight in 1994.

In 1993, after Senator Helms asked for a CIA briefing on Aristide for the Senate, he said that the CIA considered Aristide a "psychopath."

The Chicago Tribune reported that Senator Helms warned against Bill Clinton's proposed military intervention in Haiti before it was even launched.

And Senator Helms continued to criticize Aristide during Aristide's second term as President of Haiti. In December of

1990, he said: "The United States must now deal with Haiti for what it has become .... narco-traffickers, criminals and other antidemocratic elements who surround Jean-Bertrand Aristide should feel the full weight of U.S. law enforcement."

Still, the Clinton Administration continued to ignore Senator Helms' warnings throughout the 1990s. The Washington Post was also in Aristide's corner, claiming that Aristide was Haiti's only genuinely popular leader and "the only one who, if he chose to, could implement the economic and political reforms the country desperately needs. The failure of his government would likely result in another massive wave of refugees setting out for Florida."

But the liberal delusions about Aristide simply could not stand up to reality anymore. As Congressman Porter Goss said in 1999 about the Clinton Administration's support for Aristide: "If this is the crown jewel of their foreign policy successes, it says a lot about their foreign policy. The situation in Haiti is pathetic." Congressman Goss went on to point out that "[Haitian leaders] have so exhausted the patience and the aid of the friends of Haiti that even their most ardent friends are sort of worn out with the Haiti experiment."

And the Miami Herald reported "that one thing on which there is general agreement is that Aristide is currently the biggest obstacle to forward movement in Haiti. 'He's our Frankenstein,' a U.S. official ruefully observed." (May 24, 1999)

The Aristide "experiment" in Haiti has been an utter disaster, and has cost the United States billions of dollars that were sunk down the Aristide "rat hole." Senator Helms warned America about Aristide back in 1993, before Bill Clinton used the U.S. Army to put him in power, and opposed every new plan to prop up the corrupt Aristide government. If officials in Washington had only listened to Senator Helms, billions of our tax dollars could have been saved. And much of the misery of the Haitian people since 1990 might have been avoided.

Manuel Noriega

In December of 1989, the United States of America liberated the Panamanian people from the corrupt dictator Manuel Noriega. Noriega was involved in drug trafficking, arms smuggling, money laundering — as well as the ruthless oppression of his people. He also systematically violated the Panama Canal treaties and harassed U.S. military personnel in Panama.

In February 1988, Noriega was indicted in Florida on charges of drug trafficking and money laundering. Following the indictments, the United States sought to remove Noriega from power. When diplomacy and opposition parties in Panama failed to oust Noriega, military force finally became necessary. President Bush ordered 20,000 U.S. soldiers, sailors, airmen and marines to liberate Panama from Noriega and his "Dignity Battalions," armed thugs under Noriega's control. Noriega was captured, and his armed supporters were routed, but at the cost of 23 dead American servicemen.

These 23 American servicemen could have been spared if Jesse Helms had been listened to about Noriega in the first place. In 1979, Senator Helms warned about drug smuggling and corruption in Panama. Back then, the <u>Raleigh News & Observer</u> accused Senator Helms of "far-right extremism" for his warnings. As Senator Helms' campaign would declare in a 1989 campaign commercial, "Ten years have gone by and now it is clear that Senator Helms was right about the drug corruption in Panama and the <u>News & Observer</u> was wrong, again."

Back in 1986, Senator Helms stated that "it may be entirely necessary down the road" for the United States to take over the Panama Canal again if the corrupt and dangerous Noriega remained in charge. The <u>Washington Post</u> responded that Senator Helms and other "elements on the American right wing" are trying to make Noriega look bad "to make the case for going back" on the Panama Canal Treaties.

Undeterred by the <u>Washington Post</u> editorial staff, Senator Helms held hearings and continued to investigate reports about Noriega's drug running, arms trafficking and his murder of a political rival.

But equally undeterred, the <u>Washington Post</u> again attacked Senator Helms for raising the alarm about Noriega, this time in 1987. Though the <u>Post</u> admitted that "Helms did indeed start opposing Noriega long before it became fashionable to do so" (this was more than two years before the U.S. military liberation of Panama); this was not meant to be a compliment. In fact, the main point in the <u>Washington Post</u> editorial was that Helms and others were "trying to overthrow" Noriega "for reasons that aren't entirely clear."

But in December of 1989, when 20,000 American servicemen were forced to risk their lives to liberate the people of Panama from the corrupt, drug smuggling Manuel Noriega, those reasons did in fact become entirely clear — to everyone except perhaps the editorial writers at the <u>Washington Post</u>.

Saddam Hussein

Ever since the 1990 Iraqi invasion of Kuwait, Saddam Hussein has been a thorn in the side of the United States. But before Saddam's invasion of Kuwait, many American foreign policy officials were neutral or even supportive of the brutal Iraqi dictator in his conflict with Iran.

But not Senator Jesse Helms. Senator Helms had been a consistent critic of Saddam Hussein, years before the Persian Gulf War.

Back in 1988, Saddam Hussein used chemical weapons against his own Kurdish population in Iraq. Though most of the world seemed to ignore this act of barbarism, Senator Jesse Helms led the fight in the Senate to condemn "this horrible effort of the Iraqi government of systematically eradicating its own citizens of Kurdish descent."

As Senator Helms recounted on August 2, 1990, while condemning the Iraqi invasion of Kuwait, Saddam Hussein has a long track record of brutality:

> "In 1983 Iraq initiated the use of chemical weapons on its own people in the course of the war with Iran. Iraq's conduct constituted the most blatant and serious breach of the 1925 Geneva protocol banning the use of these weapons. Not even Adolf Hitler used chemical weapons in World War II. Iraq's human rights record is in the words of our State Department 'abysmal.' Iraq routinely engages in torture, arbitrary imprisonment and summary execution. And what has been the response of the United States and the world community to these outrages? The sad answer is nothing until today."

True, until the Iraqi invasion of Kuwait, nothing had been done to deal with Saddam Hussein and his evil dictatorship in Iraq. But not for lack of effort on Senator Helms' part. Years before the invasion of Kuwait, Senator Jesse Helms was warning the world about Saddam Hussein.

Here is Senator Helms, in his own words, on his thankless and lonely campaign warning against Saddam Hussein before the 1990 invasion of Kuwait:

"Over the past 2 years, a number of actions were taken here in the Senate aimed at putting a stop to Hussein's antics. Unfortunately, none of these actions became law.

On three occasions in 1988, Senator Pell and I offered amendments to impose wide-ranging sanctions on Iraq in response to Hussein's use of chemical weapons against his own civilians and against Iran in the gulf war. Unfortunately, all three amendments were killed by the House of Representatives (which was controlled by liberal Democrats).

In 1988 and again in 1989, I offered amendments to prevent any assistance to the missile program of Communist China until China stopped providing missiles to Iraq, Iran, Syria, and Libya. Unfortunately, both these amendments were killed by the House of Representatives.

On May 17 of this year, the Senate approved the chemical weapons bill, which combined S. 195 introduced by the Senator from Rhode Island and S. 238 introduced by this Senator. The bill passed by the Senate would impose sanctions on countries which use chemical weapons in violation of international law and on Western firms which help Iraq and other radical countries to gain chemical warfare capability. Unfortunately, the House of Representatives has yet to appoint conferees on this legislation.

One final point: Just last week, the Senate approved an amendment offered by the able Senator from New York [Mr. D'Amato] to the farm bill which would impose wide-ranging sanctions on Iraq. Hopefully the conferees on the farm bill will send the D'Amato amendment to the President without altering its content."

In August of 1990, the rest of the world woke up and realized what Jesse Helms had known for years about Saddam Hussein: That he was a brutal dictator and a threat to American interests in the entire Persian Gulf region. Sadly, it was too late for the United States to avoid going to war with Iraq in order to defeat Saddam Hussein. But if foreign policy leaders in Washington had heeded Senator Helms' warnings in the first place, Saddam Hussein might have been boxed in and de-fanged without our ever having to fight him in the first place.

Communist China

Since President Nixon went to China in 1972, many conservatives in the United States regarded Communist China as an ally of the United States, at least during the Cold War against the Soviet Union. But not Senator Jesse Helms. Senator Helms has been a sharp and consistent critic of Communist China from the start, and even called President Nixon's trip to Beijing in 1972 "appeasement."

During the 1980s, Senator Helms kept the pressure on Communist China. In 1982 Senator Helms fought hard for the sale of American fighter jets to Taiwan, to help them defend themselves against Communist China. And in 1985 Senator Helms held up the appointment of the U.S. Ambassador to China until he was promised that U.S. aid would not be given to countries like Communist China that forced abortion and sterilization on its people.

When the Cold War ended, the People's Republic of China was one of the few Communist countries left in the world. And even though the reason for the Sino-American alliance — opposing the Soviet Union — had ceased to exist, most Americans still considered Communist China an ally. But the truth was that Communist China was never our ally. They joined with us to bring down their immediate enemy, the U.S.S.R. But once done, Communist China immediately turned to challenge the United States for supremacy in the Pacific — and ultimately the world.

Senator Helms was one of the very few leaders in America who understood the threat we faced from Communist China. He understood the need to cooperate with Communist China against the Soviet Union. But that was as far as it went. Even during the height of the Cold War, Senator Helms was not afraid to criticize Communist China's egregious human rights record. And throughout the 1980s and 1990s, Senator Helms never let up on Communist China for proliferating weapons of mass destruction and ballistic missile technology — especially to those countries that President George W. Bush today calls an Axis of Evil: Iran, Iraq and North Korea.

Senator Helms' criticism of Communist China has not let up since President George W. Bush took office. Here is what Senator Helms had to say about Communist China and America's ally Taiwan in January, 2001, the same month President Bush took his oath of office:

"Communist China is a rising power, embarked on a massive military buildup. For 11 years running, China's military budget has increased by double digit percentages. These bulging budgets, subsidized by trade dollars from the United States and cheap loans from the World Bank, are being used to procure a raft of advanced and dangerous weaponry.

One needs only to listen to Chinese officials or read the Communist-controlled press for a day to know why China was embarked on this threatening military spending binge: the intimidation and ultimate subjugation of democratic Taiwan.

Just last month, Communist Chinese leader Jiang Zemin reportedly stated: "It is imperative to step up preparations for a military struggle so as to promote the early solution of the Taiwan issue. To this end, it is necessary to vigorously develop some 'trump card' weapons and equipment."

Make no mistake, China today is more able, and more willing, to use force against Taiwan than it was 10 years ago.

I authored the TSEA (Taiwan Security Enhancement Act), along with Sen. Robert Torricelli, precisely to redress some of the aforementioned gaps in our deterrent posture in Taiwan. The TSEA requires close consultation with Congress on defense sales to Taiwan, upgraded military ties with Taipei, the removal of restrictions on U.S. military travel to Taiwan and the establishment of better communications between our militaries.

Along with a restoration of overall U.S. military power, early implementation of the provisions of the Taiwan Security Enhancement Act by the Bush administration will be vital in lowering the chances of American men and women having to fight in the Taiwan Strait."

Though national security with regard to Communist China has always been of paramount concern to Senator Helms, economic issues have also come to dominate the debate. Many in the pro-China lobby contend that doing business with Communist China will help persuade them to move more and more toward democracy. But history shows us that no Communist government has ever evolved into a democracy, no matter what economic incentives were offered to it. And Senator Helms has always scoffed at such a notion, as he did in a September 2000 speech to Congress:

"The argument has been advanced that only by exposing the Chinese government and the Chinese people to our values through expanded trade and investment can we help bring about real political change in China. I have always been skeptical about this, because businesses are not in the business of expanding democracy.

Businesses exist to make money, and I certainly have no problem with that. But let's be honest. American businesses, even if viewed in the most charitable light, are not likely to lift a finger to promote democracy in China.

And the powerful lure of the potentially huge Chinese market has obviously clouded the judgment of some of our top companies and their executives. With regret, I have concluded that some of America's top businesses have been willing to supplicate to the Communist government of China, hoping that the Chinese government will allow them to someday make a profit there."

Senator Helms also tried to block "Most Favored" trading status for Communist China by exposing Beijing's brutal human rights record, especially when it comes to religious tolerance:

"I am pleased to support the amendment by Senator Wellstone, which simply directs the president to certify that China has met a series of religious freedom conditions prior to granting Permanent Normal Trade Relations with China. What this amendment really does is tell China, and tells the rest of the world, that we Americans still stand for something. Something other than profits, that is. And in this case, what we are saying is that we don't believe that China should be welcomed into international organizations such as the WTO while they continue to repress, jail, murder and torture their own citizens, simply for exercising their faith.

Crimes against religious believers in China abound. In the past couple of years, China has intensified its so-called patriotic re-education campaign aimed at destroying Tibetan culture and religion. Similar horror stories are taking place in the Muslim northwest. We must insist that progress on religious freedom *precede* China's entry into the WTO."

Congress failed to heed Senator Helms' warnings, and granted China Permanent "Most Favored" trading status soon after that speech. But as Senator Helms predicted, increased trade has not moved Communist China closer to democracy. In fact, since being granted "Most Favored" trade status by the United States, Communist China has pushed even harder to become the dominant power in the Pacific and opposed America's War on Terrorism at almost every step.

Communist China. Aristide, Noriega and Hussein. Senator Jesse Helms has been warning Americans about pending national security threats years before the State Department or the media discovers them. Tragically, the foreign policy "experts" did not listen at all to Senator Helms when it came to Aristide of Haiti. And they did not listen in time when it came to Manuel Noriega and Saddam Hussein. As a result, much blood was needlessly shed and a great deal of treasure was needlessly lost. So when it comes to Communist China — with the world's largest military and armed with nuclear weapons — we can only hope that Senator Helms' warnings are heeded before it is too late.

And The World Came His Way

IV
Rebuilding America's Defenses

When Ronald Reagan became the 40th President of the United States in 1981, one of his major goals was to rebuild America's defense and challenge the Soviet Union's decades of expansion. Today, with the Cold War won and the Soviet Union no more, it is clear to most that Reagan's military policies were a resounding success. But during the 1980's, President Reagan had to fight a desperate battle with anti-military "doves" and the "soft-on-communism" crowd in America, and especially with liberals in the United States Congress, to rebuild our nation's military to be able to credibly confront the Soviet Union. And Senator Jesse Helms was the one man in Congress who could be most counted upon to stand firm in favor of rebuilding America's military might — no matter whose toes he was stepping on to do it.

Rebuilding America's Military

In June of 1982, Senator Helms led the fight in Congress to increase the military defense budget as much as possible. As the Washington Post reported, "The Senate gave final congressional approval to a budget for fiscal 1983 that includes a huge military buildup program." But Senator Helms opposed this compromise budget, in part because *it did not increase military spending enough*. And over the next several years, Senator Helms was often a lonely voice in Congress standing firm for our national defense.

Senator Jesse Helms' impact on President Reagan's military buildup was far-reaching. Not only did Senator Helms help usher President Reagan's military budget requests through Congress, but he also had an impact on President Reagan's military strategy. For example, Rear Admiral James Nance, a close associate of Senator Helms, was named the Chief Military Advisor to the National Security Council. The Council, of course, was instrumental in making national security decisions in the Reagan White House.

SDI and the ABM Treaty

Probably the most critical — and divisive — national security decision to come out of the Reagan Administration was the Strategic Defense Initiative (SDI). In 1983, President Reagan proposed a missile defense system to protect the United States from nuclear attack. Senator Jesse Helms was one of the first to support President Reagan's plan. But the same liberals in Congress who opposed President Reagan's military defense buildup, opposed SDI — with a vengeance. And for the next nineteen years, these liberals tried all they could to kill President Reagan's SDI program. But thankfully, Senator Helms planted the flag in the Senate and fought tooth and nail to defend SDI.

Even before Ronald Reagan's famous SDI speech in 1983, Senator Helms fought for funding to develop a missile defense. In 1981, he sponsored an amendment asking the Senate to appropriate an additional $250 million for space lasers that could be used for missile defense.

And since 1983, Senator Helms has been the most staunch supporter of SDI. When liberals in Congress demanded that President Reagan trade SDI for an arms-control treaty in 1987, Senator Helms stood up and said that would "perpetuate the unreasonable delusion that arms-control negotiations have increased America's security."

When liberals in Congress voted to confine SDI testing to narrow limits imposed by the 1972 Anti-Ballistic Missile (ABM) Treaty in 1987, Senator Jesse Helms opposed them.

When liberals in Congress tried to kill SDI altogether in 1987 by claiming it violated the ABM Treaty, Senator Helms fought them. He called the sharp restrictions on SDI testing imposed by the liberals a victory for "liberal disarmers." Senator Helms went on to say: "The Senate needs to wake up and smell the coffee — America is in gravest mortal danger and we should abrogate the ABM Treaty because it is impeding our ability to defend our supreme national interests. SDI deployment is the name of the game, and it is absolutely essential to America's national security."

But the liberal critics of SDI — in Congress and the newspapers — have never given up in their quest to derail SDI. In 1985 the New York Times editorialized that "all four arguments [by President Reagan in favor of SDI] fail, even the moral one." It went on to call SDI "the most far-fetched yet least considered venture of the nuclear age." The Times also quoted a Pentagon scientist as saying "that the United States could not have confidence that the computer software for a 'Star Wars' defense would ever work. 'We cannot trust it', and the software for such a system would be vulnerable to 'catastrophic failure'."

Also in 1985, Liberal Congressman Edward Markey spoke for most liberals during the 1980s and 1990s when he derided SDI by saying "the President said today he would not give an inch on 'Star Wars' to get an arms control agreement. At this rate, we will probably see another ice age before we get an arms control treaty."

Helms and Reagan Were Right All Along

Liberals like Congressman Markey were dead wrong. Instead of an ice age, what we saw was victory in the Cold War over the Soviet Union — victory for President Ronald Reagan and Senator Jesse Helms.

By 1994, even the New York Times was forced to report that Ronald Reagan's vision of an SDI missile defense — outlined more than a decade before — was becoming a reality. In an article called "From Fantasy to Fact: Space Based Laser Nearly Ready to Fly," reporter William J. Broad conceded that SDI technology "is mature enough that one class of advanced weapons could be put into space relatively quickly." Broad also quoted a SDI expert as saying "Like it or hate it, this is real. It's not theoretical. It's not some scientist fantasizing about X-ray lasers." All those scientists and liberals in Congress who opposed SDI as technologically impossible finally had to face the facts — Ronald Reagan and Jesse Helms were right, and an SDI missile defense could be deployed.

It was not just that the *SDI* policy that Ronald Reagan and Jesse Helms supported so strongly worked. It was that their *entire* policy of rebuilding the military and standing tall against the Soviet Union worked. It won us the Cold War.

General Alexander Haig wrote in the Washington Post in 1996 how "Reagan revived American confidence in the rightness of our cause. His military buildup offset the long-sought Soviet bid to upset the balance of power. And his policies helped to "re-contain" a Soviet Union that was dangerously unopposed during the late 1970's." These were the policies that Jesse Helms supported.

The Tampa Tribune, in 1999, reported that "the Soviet Union's leaders took Reagan's bold plan seriously, and their understanding that they could not afford to keep pace with the United States' advancing military technology contributed to the collapse of the Soviet empire and the end of the Cold War."

Liberal columnist Richard Reeves wrote in 1999 as well, in the Denver Post, that the policies of military buildup and SDI "won the Cold War and crushed the Communists. The old conservative strategy of getting the Soviets into an arms race they did not have the economic stamina to finish can be said to have won the day." Senator Helms knew it all along.

Senator Helms' strong support of Reagan's bold defense plan helped make it happen. In December of 2001, President George W. Bush moved America closer to deployment of SDI by notifying Russia that the United States would be withdrawing from the ABM Treaty. As the Associated Press reported at the time: "With the decision, Bush takes the first step toward fulfilling a campaign pledge to develop and deploy an anti-missile system that he says will protect the United States and its allies, including Russia, from missiles fired by rogue nations. Bush has said the Sept. 11 terrorist attacks heightened the need for such a system."

So, after two decades of struggling to abrogate the ABM Treaty and deploy an SDI missile defense system, Senator Helms finally won the day in 2001, when President George W. Bush announced to the world that the United States was abrogating the ABM treaty and immediately proceeding to build and deploy an SDI missile defense to protect America from nuclear weapons. It was a long fight, but one that history will prove to be one of the most important in the defense of the United States of America.

V
Chairing Foreign Relations

The 1994 congressional elections that swept Republicans into power in both the House and Senate sent liberals into a tizzy. There were dire warnings in the liberal media about a "right wing" takeover of Congress. And no Republican scared the liberals more than Jesse Helms when he took over as Chairman of the Senate Foreign Relations Committee.

Liberals just could not stomach the idea of conservative stalwart Helms "interfering" in Bill Clinton's foreign policy initiatives. After all, Senator Helms had previously said that their precious foreign aid money was thrown down "rat holes," called Clinton's Syrian-Israeli peace accord a "fraud" and described the administration's sending of troops to Haiti to restore Jean-Bertrarde Aristide to power "disgraceful." And an official in Bill Clinton's State Department, according to the New York Times, lamented that "there is little chance that treaties on chemical weapons, biodiversity and the Law of the Sea — or nominees to serve as ambassadors to China, Israel and other countries — will pass by Mr. Helms unscathed."

That State Department official was right. Senator Helms' reign as Chairman of the Senate Foreign Relations Committee, 1995-2001, will go down in history as one of the most important in that committee's history. And Senator Jesse Helms will be recognized, not only for what he did during his reign as Chairman, but for what he prevented the Clinton Administration from doing.

William Weld

One highly publicized example of Senator Helms' importance was the 1997 nomination of William Weld to be America's Ambassador to Mexico. William Weld, a liberal Republican and governor of Massachusetts, was picked by President Clinton to be the U.S. Ambassador to Mexico in what was called "a major foreign policy stroke with a touch of political brilliance" in the <u>Chicago Tribune</u> (July 17, 1997). The Clinton Administration touted this choice as an example of bipartisanship.

But Senator Jesse Helms disapproved of Weld's lax record on drugs. He knew that Governor Weld supported the medical use of marijuana and giving needles to heroin addicts. And Senator Helms felt that someone with those positions should never become the U.S. ambassador to a country with such major drug problems.

The Clinton Administration knew they were in trouble the minute Senator Helms announced his opposition to Weld. Even ranking Democrat on the Senate Foreign Relations Committee, Senator Joe Biden, made things clear: "I think it's too early to give the last rites to the governor, but it's formidable when the chairman (Helms) takes on somebody. He has a history of demonstrating that he can hang tough." (<u>Chicago Tribune</u>, July 17, 1997)

Instead of listening to Senator Biden's warnings, William Weld and the Clinton Administration pressed forward, demanding a confirmation hearing in the Senate. But Senator Helms would not budge. He believed Governor Weld was grossly unqualified for the post of Ambassador to Mexico, and refused to even allow a hearing before the Senate Foreign Relations Committee.

Still the liberals would not give up. They forced a meeting of the Senate Foreign Relations Committee, in order to press for a confirmation hearing for Governor Weld. Still Senator Helms would not budge. And he used his authority as the Chairman of the Committee to defeat any further attempts to get a confirmation hearing, and William Weld was forced to withdraw his name for consideration as U.S. Ambassador to Mexico.

Governor Weld was not a gracious loser. He blasted Senator Helms as "a scourge on his party and U.S. government" and declared "I think Sen. Helms is where the problem is." (Fort Worth Star, September 16, 1997). Bill Clinton also chimed in, saying "the American people have not been well served."

But the American people *were* served well. And conservatives from all across the country knew it. Michael Reagan, President Ronald Reagan's son, summarized Senator Helms' unflinching stand for all conservatives:

"It's nice to see some Republicans still have a backbone. Jesse Helms showed himself to be the leader that he is. And Trent Lott supported the right person on this issue from Day One. Not only did Bill Clinton go about this nomination wrong, but he nominated the wrong person with the wrong record on drugs, and Jesse Helms and Trent Lott stood firm and said 'no'.

There are a lot of people in the Republican leadership .... who would have caved in. Maybe the leadership should look at Jesse Helms and ask why he can stand up to the pressure and they can't.

It is actions like these by Sen. Helms and Sen. Lott who stood for principle in the heat of a political battle, that appeal to grassroots Americans. If Republicans will show by their actions that they will stand on principle, they will go a long way toward rebuilding the grassroots Reagan coalition and taking back the White House."

Comprehensive Test Ban Treaty

Another example of Senator Helms' stalwart defense of American interests, even in the face of overwhelming liberal criticism, came in 1999 when President Clinton tried to get the Senate to pass his Comprehensive Test Ban Treaty. This flawed treaty purported to ban all future testing of nuclear weapons. But Senator Helms believed that testing was still necessary to ensure that America's nuclear arsenal was a safe and effective deterrent. And he knew that a bad arms control deal was worse than no arms control deal at all. Since this Comprehensive Test Ban Treaty was virtually unverifiable, countries like North Korea could cheat on it and never be caught. That would defeat the purpose of the whole treaty.

Regardless of the dangers, Democrats were intent on pressing for this treaty that would ban nuclear testing. The New York Times' front page story reports: "The White House and Senate Democrats say they are preparing for a pitched battle with the Republican-controlled Senate to save one of the top foreign policy goals of President Clinton's waning Administration: a treaty banning nuclear testing." (August 30, 1999) But Senator Helms would not let this flawed treaty even see the light of day in the Senate.

Liberals excoriated Senator Helms for bottling up the Comprehensive Test Ban Treaty. Mary McGrory of the Washington Post called Jesse Helms a "clownish senator" for not allowing a Senate vote on the treaty, and added that he "basically hates the rest of the world." (July 29, 1999) Senator Joe Biden denounced Helms' hold on the treaty as "stupid and ridiculous." (Washington Post, July 29, 1999)

But Senator Helms was undaunted by the pressure from the White House, Senate Democrats and the media. And in October of 1999, Bill Clinton was forced to give in on the Comprehensive Test Ban Treaty. Senator Helms himself said that President Clinton had to give up in this battle because "he knows he's going to get his fanny kicked" in a full Senate vote. Senator Helms had stood strong against massive pressure from the liberals, and won another victory for America's security. Washington Post reporter David Broder wrote, it was "perhaps the greatest repudiation President Clinton has suffered to his leadership since his massive health-care reform measure was shelved in 1994." (November 9, 1999)

United Nations

Jesse Helms never viewed the United Nations through rose-colored glasses, as many liberals had. The Buffalo News quoted the Senator as saying "most Americans see the United Nations as just one aspect of America's diplomatic arsenal, whose worth depends on its effectiveness in serving U.S. interests. Should the U.N. become a burden because it fails to respect the sovereign rights of the American people, the American people would cast it aside." Those remarks were "met with unanimous anger and disapproval in the Security Council." (January 30, 2000)

Senator Helms was skeptical about sending hundreds of millions of taxpayer dollars to the mismanaged United Nations — the same U.N. that more often than not took our money and spent it on policies that hurt the United States. But the Clinton Administration was intent upon paying the U.N. a billion dollars in "dues" money — with no strings attached. Senator Helms would not let them. Instead, Senator Helms demanded that the United Nations undergo a series of reforms to cut back on waste and corruption before he would allow American tax dollars to go to the United Nations.

Jesse Helms also led Senate opposition to a new International Criminal Court being cooked up at the United Nations — with support from the Clinton Administration. This new U.N. court was ostensibly to be used to put war criminals on trial. But the reality was that our enemies could use this U.N. court to put American citizens on trial — even American troops — for committing supposed "war crimes." Needless to say, the idea of our brave soldiers standing trial in front of an Iraqi or Iranian or Cuban judge did not sit well with Senator Helms. And he declared that the International Criminal Court Treaty would be "dead on arrival" in the Senate. (<u>Buffalo News</u>, January 30, 2000)

After years of hard work, Senator Helms' tireless campaign against U.N. mismanagement and anti-American policies was finally rewarded. On January 20, 2000, Senator Jesse Helms became the first legislator in history, from any country, to address the United Nations, after Senator Helms negotiated an agreement with the United Nations for long-sought reforms. And as has always been his wont, Senator Helms did not mince words with the United Nations:

"It's my hope that there can begin today a pattern of understanding and friendship between you who serve your respective countries in the United Nations, and

Telling the United Nations he wants reforms: On January 20, 2000, Senator Helms became the first legislator in history from any country to address the General Assembly.

those of us who serve not only in the United States government, but also the millions of Americans whom we represent.

It's not my intent to offend you in any way, and I hope I will not. It is my intent to extend to you my hand of friendship and convey the hope that in the days to come and in retrospect, we can join in a mutual respect that will enable all of us to work together in an atmosphere of friendship and hope — the hope to do everything we can to achieve world peace around the globe.

It may very well be that some of the things that I feel obliged to say will not meet with your immediate approval, if ever. I want the American people to value a United Nations that recognizes and respects their interests, and for the United Nations to value the significant contributions by and of the American people. And most Americans do not regard the United Nations as an end in and of itself. They see it as just one aspect of America's diplomatic arsenal. And to the extent that the United Nations is effective, the American people will support it. To the extent that it becomes ineffective, or worse, a burden, the American people, through its elected representatives, will cast it aside.

The American people see the United Nations aspiring to establish itself the central authority of a new international order of global laws and global governance. This is an international order the America people, I guarantee you, do not and will not countenance. The United Nations must respect national sovereignty in the United States and everywhere else. The United Nations serves nation-states, not the other way around. This principle is central to the legitimacy and the ultimate survival of the United Nations, and it is a principle that must be protected.

I have received literally thousands of communications from Americans all across the country, expressing their deep frustration with this institution. They know instinctively that the UN lives and breathes on the hard-earned money of the American taxpayers, among others. Yet, they have heard comments here in New York constantly calling the United States a dead-beat nation. I dissent from that and so do the American people. They have heard UN officials declaring absurdly that countries like Fiji and Bangladesh are carrying America's burden in peacekeeping. They've seen the majority of the UN members routinely voting against America in the General Assembly. They have read the reports of the raucous cheering of the UN delegates in Rome when US efforts to amend the International Criminal Court Treaty to protect American soldiers were defeated. They read in the newspapers that despite all the human rights abuses taking place in dictatorships around the globe, a UN special reporter decided that his most pressing task was to investigate human rights violations in the United States. The American people hear all of this and they resent it.

Last year, the American people contributed a total of more than $1.4 billion to the United Nations system in assessments and voluntary contributions. That's pretty generous. But it's only the tip of the iceberg. The American taxpayer also spent an additional $ 8.779 billion from the United States military budget to support various UN resolutions and peacekeeping operations around the world. No other nation on Earth comes even close to matching that investment. So you can see perhaps why many Americans reject the suggestion that their country is a deadbeat nation. And frankly, ladies and gentlemen, I resent it too.

A United Nations that focuses on helping sovereign nations work together is worth keeping; a United Nations that insists on trying to impose a utopian vision on America and the world will collapse under its own weight. If the United Nations respects the sovereign rights of the American people and serves them as an effective tool of diplomacy, it will earn their respect and support. But a United Nations that seeks to impose its presumed authority on the American people without their consent begs for confrontation and, I want to be candid, eventual US withdrawal."

U.S. Ambassador to the United Nations Richard Holbrooke called Senator Jesse Helms' U.N. visit a benchmark in the U.S.-U.N. relationship. Even Senator Joseph Biden, a Democrat from Delaware, agreed with Senator Helms' that there was a need to enact "fundamental changes" at the United Nations. "I know it. You know it. We all know it, " Biden told U.N. Secretary-General Kofi Annan. (ABC News, January 21, 2000)

But it took a leader like Senator Jesse Helms to force those fundamental changes at the United Nations. As Senator

Biden would later admit: "Just as only Nixon could go to China, only Helms could fix the U.N."

Bill Clinton's Search for a Legacy

The waning years of the Clinton Administration were a dangerous one for America. Desperate for a legacy that had nothing to do with lies, corruption and stained dresses, Bill Clinton was intent on putting his stamp on America's foreign policy — regardless of the consequences. And President Clinton felt his best chance for a "legacy" was a new arms-control agreement with Russia.

What Bill Clinton had in mind was to negotiate a massive nuclear arms reduction with Russia, and tie it to a renegotiation of the 1972 Anti-Ballistic Missile Treaty. Clinton especially liked this plan because it would not only give him an enduring legacy (or so he thought), but it would also permanently limit the deployment of an SDI missile defense system hated by the liberals. So Bill Clinton and Secretary of State Madeleine Albright set out to negotiate a deal with the Russians.

But when Senator Helms got word about this new treaty the Clinton Administration was trying to negotiate, he immediately set out to block it. "I do not intend to allow this president to establish his 'legacy' by binding the next generation of Americans to a future without viable national missile defense," said Senator Helms. "Not on my watch, Mr. President. Not on my watch."

Senator Helms later was quoted as describing Bill Clinton as "a lame duck whose 'desperate desire for a legacy' has made him so eager for an arms treaty with Russia, where Clinton is scheduled to visit in June, that he would risk U.S. security to do so." (Atlanta Journal and Constitution, May 7, 2000)

Clinton State Department spokesman James Rubin fired back at Senator Helms, by stating that he "is not the entire Senate." In response, Senator Helms simply vowed: "Let's be clear to avoid any misunderstandings: Any modified ABM Treaty negotiated by this administration will be dead on arrival at the Senate Foreign Relations Committee." (Chicago Tribune April 27, 2000)

The day after Senator Helms' remarks, the Boston Herald published an editorial praising Senator Helms for his tough stance against this arms control deal that would restrict missile defense. "The temptation to trade a no-deployment decision for Russian agreement to further missile reductions may prove irresistible to a legacy-crazed politico who did everything he could to kill missile defense for six years," the Herald editorialized, but fortunately Senator Helms won't let any such treaty out of committee. What a relief!" (April 28, 2000)

Restructuring the State Department

But not all of Senator Jesse Helms' work as Chairman of the Senate Foreign Relations Committee was saying "NO" to the Clinton Administration. Senator Helms also pushed his own agenda in the Senate, including legislation that would institute a long-sought restructuring of the State Department. Agreed upon in 1997, the Foreign Affairs Reform and Restructuring Act was passed in 1998, and went into effect October 1, 1999.

Though this restructuring of the State Department was not as dramatic as Senator Helms' showdown with Governor Weld or the defeat of the Comprehensive Test Ban Treaty, it may well prove to be one of Jesse Helms' greatest legacies. In this restructuring, Senator Helms succeeded in absorbing both the U.S. Information Agency and the Arms Control and Disarmament Agency into the State Department. It also directed the Agency for International Development to report to the State Department, rather than the President directly.

Senator Helms believed that America's foreign affairs bureaucracy was outdated. Mostly a relic of the Cold War, the U.S. foreign policy bureaucracy had become terribly unwieldy, often preventing the United States from forming and administering a coherent policy. Senator Helms also believed that most foreign aid was a waste of America's tax dollars because the aid itself did little or nothing to advance America's interests.

The State Department restructuring went a long way toward solving these problems. Layers of duplicate bureaucracy were eliminated at both agencies, which saved millions of tax dollars. More importantly, the U.S. Arms Control, Information and Foreign Aid agencies are all now under the direction of the Secretary of State. Before, these agencies did not always cooperate and coordinate. Now, the Secretary of State coordinates America's arms control, information and foreign aid programs as one single and coherent policy. As a result, America's foreign policy is now more efficient and effective at pressing U.S. interests abroad.

Senator Helms received nearly universal praise for his long struggle to restructure America's foreign policy establishment. The Overseas Development Council said in an April 24, 1997 article entitled "Reorganization: A Good Decision" that: "Helms is right that the foreign aid machinery constructed to wage the Cold War is outdated, and that a reorganization would suit the foreign policy requirements of the post-Cold War era." Even liberal Senator Ted Kennedy took the time to praise the restructuring of the State Department that Senator Helms had brought about. "It is a significant and quantum improvement on communications so the U.S. Government communicating overseas can match the speed and accuracy that U.S. domestic news services have," said Kennedy.

It may not have been as exciting or controversial as a key confirmation hearing or a showdown over treaty ratification, but the Foreign Affairs Reform and Restructuring Act is one of Senator Helms' most important accomplishments as chairman of the Senate Foreign Relations Committee.

Legacy as Chairman

Senator Jesse Helms has been critical to the foreign policy process in America during his reign as Chairman of the Senate Foreign Relations Committee. He acted as both unflappable defender of core principles and pragmatic compromiser with ranking Democrat Joe Biden and Clinton Secretary of State Madeleine Albright.

As Patricia McNerney, the Republican Chief of Staff for the Senate Foreign Relations Committee, noted:

"The Helms-Albright and Helms-Biden relationships were key to the success of Senator Helms' chairmanship. His ability to form coalitions transcending politics really placed Senator Helms in the role of statesman in the Senate. As a result of working with both Albright and Biden, he was able to achieve a lasting legislative legacy."

It is true that, in just a brief time, historians have looked back on Senator Helms' reign as Senate Foreign Relations Committee Chairman and noted what a critical role he played.

"Presidents and secretaries of state court the powerful Senator Helms the way Harry S. Truman and Dean Acheson courted Senator Arthur H. Vandenberg in the 1940's — or curse his name the way Lyndon B. Johnson and his secretary of state, Dean Rusk, cursed Senator J. William Fulbright during the Vietnam War. But while hating Jesse Helms remains a parlor sport in Georgetown, Cambridge and Manhattan, a longer view of American history would demonstrate that Jesse Helms is a necessary part of the process: If he did not exist, America would have to invent him." So wrote Walter Russel Mead of the Council on Foreign Relations, in a New York Times editorial at the end of Helms' reign as the Senate Foreign Relations Committee Chairman. In the same Times piece, historian Douglas Brinkley is quoted as saying: "You have to have both yin and yang in American foreign policy, and Jesse Helms provides the yang. You can't sway Helms ideologically, but you can work out a pragmatic agenda if you can meet his basic concerns. He respects his hard-line constituency but is willing to explore centrist possibilities. This is what makes him so important to the foreign-policy process."

And The World Came His Way

VI
Driving the Flat Tax Bandwagon

In 1996, presidential candidate Steve Forbes spent tens of millions of dollars promoting his proposal for a flat tax. Forbes ran television ad after television ad extolling the virtues of a single tax rate for all Americans — without the rules and regulations of the IRS. He was called "Johnny-one-note" by some for his single-issue campaign. Another wag said, "ask him about abortion and the answer is the flat tax." But, the flat tax concept was embraced by Republican primary voters all over the country. Forbes, a less than smooth campaigner with no political background, came from out of nowhere to nearly derail Bob Dole's quest for the Republican nomination.

While the media focused a lot of its coverage of Forbes on the amount of money he was spending, the real point was the issue of the flat tax was popular with Republican voters.

Senator Phil Gramm, another candidate for the 1996 GOP presidential nomination, also touted the virtues of the flat tax during his campaign. Simultaneously, House Majority Leader Richard Armey was touring the country promoting the flat tax. Armey said: "Our nation's tax code is in dire need of a major overhaul. The tax code is a costly, complicated and burdensome monstrosity that cannot be tamed by any amount of tinkering or fine tuning."

> "Armey and Forbes are getting a lot of attention, but I don't know that the flat tax would have advanced as far as it has without people like Helms who were willing to keep the flame alive."
>
> **Daniel Mitchell**
> *Senior Fellow, Heritage Foundation*

Senator Jesse Helms has been a leading proponent in Washington of the flat tax — since 1982.

In a story during the 1996 presidential campaign entitled "Helms, 'flat tax godfather,' has backed cause for years", the Raleigh <u>News & Observer</u> wrote:

> "Senator Jesse Helms has a Tar Heel greeting for everyone jumping on the flat-tax bandwagon these days: Welcome aboard, y'all. With various Republican presidential candidates, senators and congressmen pushing different tax simplification plans, the idea of a flat tax is suddenly all the rage. For Helms, though, it's an old cause. He has introduced flat tax legislation five times since 1982, most recently in July."

Indeed, Helms introduced S. 2200 the Flat Rate Tax Act of 1982 on March 15th of that year. In a Senate floor speech on June 29th, Senator Helms further outlined the reasoning behind his support for the flat tax:

"I am concerned that the solution to our current economic problem — and most of the economic problems around the world — lies in the adoption of policies that will foster growth and prosperity. I do not believe that burdening the American worker with higher taxes will promote more output or production.

The reason that the flat-rate tax would not lead to revenue loss is that it would significantly broaden the tax base by closing exemptions, except for a $2,000 basic individual exemption. At present only about 70 percent of total income is taxable....

When one adds to the underground economic activity all the legal forms of tax avoidance — shelters, preferences, exemptions, et cetera — the result is that for every dollar paid in individual taxes, 57 cents is not paid according to an Evans Economics study....

Our present tax system is the ugly stepchild of the Congress and advocates of special interest legislation. The complexities of our tax codes are mind-boggling — nearly 52 percent of the 1040 forms and 16.9 percent of the "simple" 1040A were filled out with professional assistance in 1981, and even then over half of the itemized returns contained mistakes according to the IRS. This complexity is especially unfair to those who cannot afford to pay for the services of a professional tax accountant.

Our present tax system is unworkable and intolerable. The need for a complete overhaul of the system should be obvious to everyone — the problem is not solved by piecemeal reform, which can only add to confusion and inefficiency. We should wipe the slate clean of tax preferences, deductions, exemptions, exclusions and all other complicating factors. We must make the philosophical stand that the flat rate across-the-board tax rate is the only possible solution to our tax systems' inequities and inefficiencies."

With those words, spoken in 1982, Senator Jesse Helms laid out the framework and the basic arguments for the flat tax. Many others would later pick up the torch and carry it forward. Indeed it will be for another generation to ultimately pass a flat tax. But Jesse Helms was instrumental in getting the flat tax movement started.

Several 1982 news articles chronicle Helms' role in the genesis of the flat tax. New York Times columnist William Safire discussed Senator Helms' plan for a flat tax in an April 30, 1982 column. Safire's column reported:

"Senator Jesse Helms, the ultra-traditionalist has dropped a bill in the Senate hopper spelling out a Flat Rate Tax Act of 1982. The flat tax is neither a tax on flatness nor a levy on apartments in London. The idea is to do away with tax brackets gradually going up to 50 percent of earnings, and to discard as well the current rabbit warren of tax shelters, loopholes and special credits .... the Helms proposal is for a flat 10 percent and a $2,000-per-person allowance."

In a May 25, 1982 article, "Flat Income Tax Gaining advocates", the New York Times wrote: "The flat tax has received support from conservatives like Senator Jesse Helms, Republican of North Carolina and liberals like Leon E. Panetta, Democrat of California." The Christian Science Monitor in September of 1982 acknowledged Senator Helms' role in the flat tax movement in the first paragraph of its commentary on the flat tax:

"The flat tax is, if nothing else, startling. It has evoked enthusiasm from such disparate individuals as Ralph Nader and Jesse Helms, plus signs of interest from the Reagan Administration."

The economic counsel to Senator Robert Kasten, Elise Payan, drafted the essay "Flat Tax Legislation in the 98th Congress" (1983-1984)). A 1984 Human Events article describes her report this way: "Quoting Senator Jesse Helms (R-N.C.), Ms. Payan lists the features a 'true' flat-tax proposal should include:

- Income should be taxed only once
- Income should be taxed at the same low rate for all individuals
- The flat tax should have a broad tax base with tax deductions, credits or exemptions

- Personal exemptions should be maintained for those with special needs, e.g. the poorest households, families with handicapped or elderly members"

It is clear that Jesse Helms defined the terms of the flat-tax debate in the early 1980's.

In a 1996 Raleigh News & Observer article, leaders of the Heritage Foundation (a leading conservative think tank in Washington) acknowledged Helms' pivotal role in bringing the flat tax to national prominence. The News & Observer remarked:

"One of the longtime institutional promoters of a flat tax is the Heritage Foundation, a conservative bastion of 'supply-side economics,' the Reagan-era theory that cutting taxes increases government revenue by fueling economic activity.

Daniel J. Mitchell, a senior fellow at Heritage, says Helms laid the groundwork for current flat-tax advocates such as House Majority Leader Richard Armey and GOP presidential candidates Steve Forbes and Phil Gramm:

'Armey and Forbes are getting a lot of attention, but I don't know that the flat tax would have advanced as far as it has without people like Helms who were willing to keep the flame alive,' Mitchell says. 'A lot of the others are Johnny-come-latelies.'"

The News & Observer concluded that "the recent eruption of interest in a flat tax is another example of current political orthodoxy in Washington moving closer to views Helms has had for years."

And The World Came His Way

VII
Seeking a Solution To Social Security

In the early 1980s, the Social Security system was teetering on the verge of bankruptcy. President Ronald Reagan appointed a bi-partisan commission to deal with the Social Security crisis. Like most bi-partisan commissions in Washington, the 1982-83 "National Commission on Social Security Reform" proposed a "status quo, raise taxes, cut benefits a little" plan.

Senator Jesse Helms said the plan "reflects a total absence of creativity and imagination." So Helms introduced his own plan to rescue Social Security. He even took the unusual step of taping a 30-minute speech on his proposal that was broadcast on TV stations throughout North Carolina. Other politicians took the easy route and hid under the cover of the bi-partisan commission to protect themselves from the politically lethal Social Security bullet.

But here was Senator Helms, facing the biggest election contest of his career against the most popular Democratic politician in the history of North Carolina, challenging the conventional wisdom on Social Security and touching this "third rail" of American politics — just because it was the right thing to do.

Predictably, the North Carolina Democratic Party wasted no time in pouncing on the Helms plan. At a state Democratic Party news conference, liberal Democratic Congressman Charlie Rose said Helms' plan "will throw the nation's elderly and widows to the mercy of the money markets and make the United States government guarantee the results." Another North Carolina Democrat, Congressman Stephen Neal, said: "It's the same idea as making Social Security voluntary. This program simply won't work." (Raleigh Times, January 28, 1983)

But others, like the Goldsboro News Argus, defended Jesse Helms for having the courage to step forward and lead on the combustible issue of Social Security. The News Argus said:

> "Social Security has been used by irresponsible politicians to bludgeon their opponents and frighten the public, especially those dependent upon it .... The issue has been met with a combination of cowardice and misleading and unproductive rhetoric.

> What the nation desperately needs today is someone in Congress with the courage to come to grips with the deeply troubled program that affects more people — contributors and beneficiaries — than any other in the country.

> We need someone willing to offer a program which because of the problem it addresses will be politically perilous if not fatal.

We need someone with the perception, the courage and the honesty to outline a solution and fight for it at all costs.

He [Helms] has demonstrated a willingness — a determination — to stand on his convictions and principle at whatever political cost.

No other member of Congress has so championed the cause of fiscal integrity in government, the element disastrously missing in our Social Security program.

Senator Helms, and perhaps he alone, can provide the rare brand of leadership we so desperately need on this issue today.

Jesse Helms may be the only elected official in Washington with sufficient statesmanship to be willing to place his political future on the altar of sacrifice by leading us out of the wilderness on Social Security." (January 16, 1983)

Even some anti-Helms newspapers like the Fayetteville Times credited Senator Helms with trying to advance the public debate on the issue. In an editorial entitled "Two Temerity Awards," the Times opined that "Helms proposes converting the Social Security system to a tax deductible private retirement account system .... He is acting with temerity (rashness or foolish boldness in the best sense) to offer an alternative. Kick it down, or up, or around. But give him a T for trying, too."

On March 16, 1983, Senator Jesse Helms outlined his "Social Security Guarantee and Individual Retirement Security Act of 1983," in a lengthy speech on the floor of the U.S. Senate. Excerpted below are some of the highlights of this groundbreaking speech on Social Security:

> "We will be deceiving ourselves if we do not face up to the seriousness of the Social Security crisis. In my view, it is both a national tragedy and a national disgrace. What is more, too few Americans understand the nature and extent of these problems. Certain politicians and members of the media have made a political football out of Social Security.
>
> Let us examine for a moment how so many Americans have been misled, even deceived, by political and bureaucratic words and phrases that have created false impressions in their minds. To put it bluntly, the people have been hoaxed by expressions that have crept into the American vocabulary.
>
> First, how many times have we heard references to the "Social Security Trust Fund"? There is no trust fund. It does not exist. It has never existed. Just ask someone to point out the vault where the money is kept. From the first days of Social Security, the American people have been led to believe that every worker has an accumulated savings account in Washington with his or her name on it. That is what

the employer and employee payroll taxes were supposed to be paying for. But such accumulated savings accounts do not exist, they never existed.

Second, how many times have American workers been told that they "contribute" a specified sum of money to Social Security, and their employer "contributes" a like amount? But that is not correct either. All of the money-what workers contribute and what employers contribute-all of it is a part of the total payroll expenses that an employer has allotted for a particular job, including salary and other costs involved in his having hired someone in the first place. So every penny is really the worker's money, the money an employer has to pay in a dozen different ways to employ someone.

So, Mr. President, that contribution is not a contribution. It is a tax, and nothing more. Social Security, as it now exists, is not really a retirement insurance and savings program. It is a program of taxation that is in fact bankrupt; and the retirement benefits of every American are, and have been, at the mercy of politicians who decide how much money from the Federal Treasury retired Americans will receive.

In the long run, Mr. President, I would phase in a new kind of private savings account, called an individual retirement security account (IRSA), in which each working American could invest for his or her own retirement. These federally insured accounts would guarantee for all time absolute retirement security for every American. They would also help the Nation's economy by creating a capital pool for investment to create jobs and put people back to work, lower interest rates, boost GNP, and help this Nation toward a much needed economic recovery.

My plan would authorize every American worker to establish an "Individual Retirement Security Account" in whatever authorized institution he or she chooses, be it a local bank, credit union, savings and loan association, or whatever. These fiduciaries would be qualified under standards similar to those under Treasury Regulations section 1.41-12(n). This new kind of account would be similar to the IRA accounts most people know about already, but with a big difference. The difference would be that a tax credit, instead of a tax deduction, would be given for deposits in these individual retirement security accounts. A tax credit means a dollar-for-dollar tax writeoff, the kind that means something to the small and medium-income taxpayer.

Individuals could contribute to these IRSA's any amounts they choose. For every dollar contributed to an IRSA, the individual would be entitled to claim a 20-cents-on-the-dollar credit against the income tax liability, up to a maximum credit of 20 percent of the amount paid that year by the individual to the Social Security trust fund. To the extent the individual elects to take advantage of the income tax credit, his future pension claims against the common Social Security trust fund would be reduced according to an actuarial formula. Maximum utilization of the income tax credit each year for 20 years would reduce the individual's OASI claims to zero. Lesser utilization would reduce the trust fund's liabilities proportionately.

My proposal would guarantee all the current pension obligations with the full faith and credit of the United States. Many Americans are surprised when they learn that Social Security benefits are not guaranteed under current law. In fact, in 1960, the U.S. Supreme Court ruled in *Fleming v. Nestor* (363 U.S. 603) that the Federal Government can renege on Social Security benefits at any time. That case is still the law today. If Congress wants to reduce Social Security benefits, it is free to do so. I want to change that.

Under my plan, every participant, upon retirement, would receive a certificate made out in his or her name. It would be an obligation backed by the "full faith and credit of the United States." This bond would guarantee continued Social Security benefits. Never again will a retired American feel that his or her Social Security benefits would be cut by an act of

Congress, the courts, or any other agency of Government. No one could ever be denied the credits he or she has earned or will earn in the future under the Government system.

Everyone's retirement credits must be guaranteed.

Interest, dividends, and capital gains accumulated in the IRSA account would be tax exempt, and annuities and withdraws from it upon retirement anytime after age 62 would be tax free. Funds held in an IRSA account could be used tax free by a worker before age 62 to acquire life insurance, health insurance, or disability insurance. The individual could participate with his fiduciary in managing the IRSA account as a fully funded individual retirement program.

My proposal also addresses the short-term financing crisis facing the Social Security system. Undeniably, a short-term infusion of funds is needed to keep the system afloat, at least until my long-range plan has a chance to take effect. The Commission estimates a deficit of from $150 to $200 billion between now and 1989. They propose to raise $168 billion through a combination of tax increases and benefit cuts. Using the Commission's own numbers and assumptions, I have come up with a package of proposals and reforms that will yield $167 billion in additional revenues between now and 1989. Quite frankly, my proposals

Senator Bob Dole

"Senator Helms took the courageous position of offering his own comprehensive reform bill which aimed at reducing the tax burden and planning for private retirement.

Senator Helms addresses head-on the major retirement income policy questions which have been ignored for a long time.

Certainly the distinguished Senator from North Carolina was willing to face the challenge to take a fresh approach to Social Security reform."

should actually yield more than this because of the favorable effect on employment of my proposed tax cut. With lower taxes and greater savings, the economy will grow faster than the Commission assumes, thus boosting the tax base and lowering benefit outflows.

The first thing I propose to do is to include all Federal workers under Social Security — not just new ones, as the Commission has proposed — but all of them, beginning with all Members of Congress and their staffs. The Social Security problem is a national problem, and all of us ought to participate in solving the crisis.

My proposal would not affect the civil service retirement system in any way. Federal employees could continue to participate in civil service retirement much the same way employees in the private sector participate in their employer-sponsored retirement plans.

Second, I propose to delay for 3 months — from July to October — the Social Security cost-of-living adjustment. I do not agree that there should be a 6-month delay, as was proposed by the Commission. That is an unfair burden on our senior citizens. A 3-month delay would be much fairer, and it would help a great deal to solve the short-term deficit.

Third, cost-of-living increases should be prorated to reflect the month of retirement. The present system is unfair to the senior citizen who retires in, say, January — because the person who retires the following December now receives the same cost-of-living adjustment as the senior citizen who retired early in the year.

Fourth, I propose that the expenses of administering the Social Security system be counted against general revenues rather than the Social Security accounts. Payroll tax revenues should only be used to pay benefits, and should not go to pay administrative expenses.

Fifth, I propose we adopt the Commission's recommendations regarding crediting the Social Security system for all uncashed Social Security checks. Until I began my detailed study of the Social Security system, I was not aware that millions of dollars in Social Security checks are never cashed each year. I was astonished to learn that the money represented by these uncashed checks does not have to go back to the Social Security system — but instead may be used for other Government spending. My proposal would require that the money be credited to the Social Security system.

Sixth, I propose the Social Security fund also be credited for all military benefits the Social Security system pays out with no Government contribution.

Mr. President, along with proposals for solving the long-term and short-term funding problems facing the Social Security system, my bill also contains proposals for reforming Social Security in certain areas. I include these reform proposals because of the pressing need for Congress to address issues relating to women, the disabled, nonresident aliens, and older Americans with productive abilities who wish to continue working past age 65.

Mr. President, clearly our present Social Security system treats women unfairly. The problems have become more acute as more women have entered the workforce. When the Social Security system was created, only 20 percent of women were in the work force. Today, that figure is roughly 60 percent.

First, present law permits the continuation of benefits for surviving spouses who remarry after age 60. This would be extended to disabled surviving spouses aged 50 to 59, disabled divorced surviving spouses aged 50 to 59, and divorced surviving spouses aged 60 or over.

Second, spouse benefits for divorced spouses would be payable at age 62 or over, subject to the requirement that the divorcee has lasted for a significant period, if the former spouse is eligible for retirement benefits, whether or not they have been claimed, or if they have been suspended because of substantial employment.

Third, deferred surviving-spouse benefits would continue to be indexed as under present law, except that the indexing would be based on the increases in wages after the death of the worker instead of by the increases in the CPI, as under present law.

Fourth, the benefits rate for disabled widows and widowers aged 50 to 59 at disablement would be the same as that for nondisabled widows and widowers first claiming benefits at age 60 — that is, 71 ½ percent of the primary insurance amount — instead of the lower rates under present law — gradually rising from 50 percent at age 50 to 71 ½ percent for disablement at age 60.

I also propose extending additional equity to divorced spouses. Both members of a household should be considered to have made equal contributions to their family and thus retain equal property rights for the income in their family structure. This is not the case under Social Security today. My legislation would correct this situation by crediting each divorced spouse half the earned family income during the marriage for the purpose of determining Social Security retirement and disability benefits.

I would be the first to acknowledge that there has been much abuse of Social Security disability. But the movement to correct this situation must have guidelines and it must be fair. Therefore, I propose that Congress insure due process to every individual receiving disability benefits before any benefits can be cut off. My bill provides this. Each disability beneficiary would be entitled to a hearing before an administrative law judge before benefits could be cut. The Social Security Administration could not bring a case before a judge for determination unless they could show a change of circumstances or conditions affecting the individual, fraud, or mistake in the initial determination of disability.

And finally, Mr. President, I propose a reform of utmost importance. I propose elimination of the earnings limit on retired persons.

Mr. President, the retirement security of American workers is as important to the future of this country as any issue Congress will deal with this year. Sooner or later, a plan such as I have proposed will have to be adopted. It may not happen this year, or even next. Eventually, the politicians will no longer be able to paper over the enormous deficit. As fewer and fewer workers support more and more retirees, Members of Congress will be unable to duck the long-term funding problems. All else having failed, they will be obliged to turn to common sense."

After Senator Helms' floor speech, Senator Bob Dole remarked:

"Senator Helms took the courageous position of offering his own comprehensive reform bill which aimed at reducing the tax burden and planning for private retirement.

As he pointed out in his statement on the floor, the Senator from Kansas thinks the bill which the Senate Finance Committee reported, is an improvement on the Commission's recommendations. There were incorporated in that bill about 11 of the provisions the Senator from North Carolina had in his

comprehensive package. Senator Helms addresses
head-on the major retirement income policy questions
which have been ignored for a long time. Obviously,
he has used the current funding crisis as much more
than an opportunity for patching up the financing
problem. Certainly the distinguished Senator from
North Carolina was willing to face the challenge to
take a fresh approach to Social Security reform."

Unfortunately, Senator Jesse Helms' plan was not
followed back in 1983, or for many years after that. Instead,
Congress took the easy way out — it kept on raising taxes
and cutting benefits rather than reforming the Social Security
system. By the year 2000, the collapse of the Social Security
system was in sight.

GOP presidential candidate George W. Bush proposed to
overhaul the Social Security system during the presidential
elections. And Senator Jesse Helms' Social Security plan in
1983 was in many ways the forerunner of George W. Bush's
plan in 2000. Like Jesse Helms, George Bush did not want to
just raise taxes for Social Security. "We cannot tax our way
to reform," declared Bush. (CNN, August 1, 2000) George
Bush also proposed investing a portion of Social Security in
the stock market.

And The World Came His Way

VIII
Balancing the Budget
'Senator No' Says Yes to Future Generations

During his tenure in the Senate, Jesse Helms continually warned about the consequences of big government spending. Helms fought against excessive government spending in many areas, including foreign aid, the United Nations, food stamps, federal education funding, and the National Endowment for the Arts.

In the early 1980s, Senator Helms used his position as Chairman of the Senate Agriculture Committee to reduce the growth of the fraud-ridden food stamp program. He strongly believed that the Carter Administration had allowed the program to run out of control. Numerous news accounts of misuse of the program, combined with the fact that this was one program where the average citizen could see the abuse of a government program in the grocery check-out line, led to a backlash against the program. Helms simply gave voice to the public outrage over the corruption in the food stamp program.

The foreign aid budget was another area of concern to Senator Helms — and he used his position on the Foreign Relations Committee to slow the growth of foreign aid. The Senator and his advisors were continually amazed that the foreign policy establishment could not justify the dollar amounts for what it was asking. Admiral James (Bud) Nance, Helms' boyhood friend who served as Republican Staff Director of the Foreign Relations Committee from 1992 until his death in 1999, once went on a search to find out why the U.S. was giving Russia $1 billion. The money was ostensibly for dismantling nuclear warheads. But Nance wanted to know: "How did they come up with the figure of $1 billion? Why isn't it $900 million or $1.2 billion?" Nance went on to point out: "I searched all around town and nobody could give us an answer to the question." The lack of coherent explanation for how funds were spent led Senator Jesse Helms to oppose many government spending programs.

Senator Helms felt that waste and abuse in government spending was systemic. On several occasions, he offered amendments to cut government spending across the board. For instance, during debate over the 1984 budget (in May of 1983), Senator Helms introduced legislation to cut all federal spending by 10 percent. The only exceptions would be for defense, Social Security and interest on the national debt. The Helms 10% Amendment lost on a 59-41 vote in the Senate.

So Senator Helms followed up with a second amendment that would have cut all government spending except defense, Social Security and interest on the debt by a meager 5%. The 5% Amendment received more votes (45), but still went down to defeat 55-45.

While many of Senator Helms' specific amendments to cut spending went down to defeat, he was winning the overall philosophical battle about the dangers of excessive government spending. The 1984 Republican Party Platform on government spending reads like a Helms speech:

"The role of the federal government should be limited. We reaffirm our conviction that state and local governments closest to the people are the best and most efficient. President Reagan has done much to alleviate federal regulatory and bureaucratic burdens on individuals and businesses. Congress has failed to act. The size and scope of the federal government remains much too large and must be reduced."

Senator Helms' fight to reduce government spending necessarily entailed voting against a lot of individual government spending programs — some of which were politically popular. Helms was definitely not one of the phony, plastic politicians who gave political speeches bemoaning the federal deficit, but then voted for spending increases in every government program in town.

All these votes against popular spending programs were easy cannon fodder for Helms' Democratic opponents. During the 1984 U.S. Senate race, Governor Jim Hunt repeatedly attacked Senator Helms for Helms' votes against big government.

Hunt told the Atlanta Journal "the man's voting record is abysmal. He's voted directly against the interests of 75 to

80% of the people, and we're going to get that message across." (May 20, 1984)

At a partisan Democratic rally in North Carolina, Hunt declared that Helms "is a man whose public career has been spent opposing those values we believe in. He's voted against us, our children, our elderly, education, fair taxes for the working people, Social Security, medicare, and the farmer." (Mount Olive Tribune, June 5, 1984)

Senator Helms' challenger in 1990 and 1996, Harvey Gantt, used similar irrational rhetoric to bash Jesse Helms' voting record:

"You're not observing that Mr. Helms is doing anything for your child or your children, for your grandmother, for the economy of North Carolina, for protecting the environment .... for improving the quality of food inspection. He's one of the people who have voted against improving standards for inspected meat." (Carolina Peacemaker, November 2, 1995)

In 1996, Senator Helms made clear that his votes against big government were to protect future generations. After Harvey Gantt kept promising everything to everybody, Helms declared: "He's got a new idea to spend more of your money and pile more debt on your children and your grandchildren." (Dallas Morning News, October 20, 1996)

But to hear Helms' opponents tell it, ole Jesse was against everything from "the farmer" to "your grandmother" to "quality food." But in the end, North Carolina voters never fell prey to the inane verbiage that emanated from his foes during election years.

North Carolina's common sense voters understood that the nation could not continue to spend unlimited amounts of money on every single program — and balance the budget.

Voters on the national level eventually began to tell politicians of all stripes that they were tired of the special interest, big government policies of the past. Then, President Bill Clinton proclaimed in his 1996 State of the Union Address that "the era of big government is over."

Even Jesse Helms' longtime nemesis, the Raleigh News and Observer, acknowledged that Senator Helms had carried the day in framing the debate over government spending:

"No statement could have made Helms happier than Clinton's declaration in his State of the Union Address this year, 'The era of big government is over.'

Helms' ideas that caught on:

The bipartisan competition to reduce the scope of the federal government has produced movement on various domestic issues Helms has championed for decades. The Republican-controlled Congress has a seven-year plan for balancing the budget. The House approved a balanced-budget amendment last year, while the Senate failed to do so by a single vote.

Clinton is battling the Republicans on where the spending cuts should fall, but several agencies that Helms has long derided as liberal symbols are targeted for reductions, including the Legal Services Corporation, the National Endowment for the Arts and the Public Broadcasting Service."

It seems nearly everyone now wanted to at least be <u>seen</u> as being "Senator No" when it came to big government.

IX
Five Elections, Five Victories
Helms' Issue-based Campaigns Transform American Politics

Jesse Helms' successful career as a TV commentator on WRAL in Raleigh had been built on discussing issues in a straightforward manner. So it was not surprising that Senator Helms' campaigns were also issues-based and ideologically-driven. Senator Helms and his political strategists strongly believed that campaigns based solely on political party and personality did little to inform the voter. Senator Helms' campaigns routinely used issues like taxes, government spending, national defense and affirmative action to drive voters to the polls. The theory was simple: Give the person who was <u>not</u> a straight party voter a reason to go vote for Jesse Helms.

In addition, registered Democrats out numbered registered Republicans in Senator Helms' five races. So Senator Helms had no choice but to make issue-oriented appeals to conservative Democrats and independents to encourage these voters to vote for a Republican candidate.

1972 Helms vs. Galifinakis
Helms Becomes First GOP Senator from
North Carolina since Reconstruction

Jesse Helms was first elected to the U.S. Senate in 1972. Helms left his longtime job at WRAL-TV to make a long-shot run for the U.S. Senate. No Republican had been elected to the U.S. Senate from North Carolina in the 20th Century.

The base of the Democratic Party was in Eastern North Carolina — before Jesse Helms entered politics. However, Helms' strongest following on WRAL-TV was also in the eastern part of the state. Helms was able to convert these conservative Democratic <u>viewers</u> into <u>voters</u> for Helms. Helms won his first race by 118,000 votes, defeating Congressman Nick Galifinakis.

There is no question that the Richard Nixon landslide of 1972 played a major role in Helms' first election victory. Nixon received 70% of the vote in North Carolina against liberal Democratic presidential candidate George McGovern. The Nixon and Helms victories in North Carolina demonstrated that this state's voters would choose philosophy if given a clear choice between a conservative Republican and a liberal Democrat.

1978 Helms vs. Ingram
Senator Helms' Easiest Re-election Race

In 1978, Senator Helms faced off against maverick
insurance commissioner, John Ingram. Ingram was not
popular among the Democratic party establishment — and he
became even less popular among the Democratic faithful after
he defeated their candidate, Luther H. Hodges, Jr. in the
primary. Helms raised $7.5 million for his 1978 race and he
was never seriously challenged by Ingram. Senator Helms
cruised to a 55-45 victory in November 1978.

1984 Helms vs. Hunt
Biggest Senate Race in U.S. History

The 1984 campaign between Jesse Helms and North
Carolina Governor Jim Hunt may very well have been the
biggest Senate race in U.S. history. Helms started the race 17
points behind. A full year before the election, the media had
already begun celebrating Jesse Helms' demise. A
Washington Post story written by a former reporter for the
Raleigh News & Observer was headlined: "Helms has a
problem; he's destined to lose in '84". The article declared
that "it will be no contest" and "barring an act of God, Helms
can't win" and "it's all over but the shouting."

Senator Helms' back was against the wall like never
before. And, once again, he won by almost 100,000 votes.
Many people have described the 1984 Helms campaign as the
best run U.S. Senate race in history for overcoming such a
huge margin against a very formidable opponent.

Some in the media wrote stories critical of the tenor of the campaign. But never were Shakespeare's words more appropriate: They "doth protest too much, methinks." The media had looked forward to this race between North Carolina's two political powerhouses just as much as the candidates and their advisors. At least, the <u>Durham Morning Herald</u> was honest enough to admit it. In a June 19, 1983 editorial entitled "Political Gladiators Promise A Slugfest," the <u>Herald</u> proclaimed:

> "The all-but-certain opponents are U.S. Senator Jesse Helms, the Republican, and Governor Jim Hunt, the Democrat, two men whose political ambitions are insatiable, whose views are irreconcilable and whose strategies should treat us to a joust that will shock and provoke ....

> To date, there is no calm middle ground in the Helms-Hunt fight. They are in their corners, teasing us with glares that promise a slugfest ....

> But you ain't seen nothing yet.

> This is just preliminary sparring to what may be one of the greatest political matches in North Carolina history. Indeed, it is likely to be a fight of national significance.

> Hurry, ring the bell."

This __Raleigh News & Observer__ cartoon depicts the raucous third debate between Senator Helms and Governor Hunt during the 1984 campaign.

In a second editorial, on October 29, 1983, the Durham Morning Herald again called for Hunt and Helms to get *tougher* with each other. The Herald's editorial (which ran nearly six months after the beginning of the Helms' TV ad campaign against Hunt) was entitled "Kindle the Hunt-Helms Fire." The Herald editorial proclaimed:

> "Senator Jesse Helms has written a personal letter to Governor Jim Hunt, challenging Mr. Hunt to television debates — 'a friendly discussion of issues.'
>
> Please, gentlemen, have your debates but spare us a 'friendly discussion.' North Carolina wants some fireworks out of both candidates: the conservative Mr.

Helms, the moderate-to-liberal Mr. Hunt. Tar Heel voters want quotes that burn, viewpoints that clash, candidates who will howl about how important their views are.

And no one is more suitable to a bombastic campaign that will clearly identify the differences between its participants than Mr. Hunt and Mr. Helms ....

On real issues — the economy, defense spending, educational reform, social legislation — Mr. Helms and Mr. Hunt would be hard put to give voters a friendly discussion. They don't see eye-to-eye, even eye-to-toe.

To be fair to North Carolina voters, they must do battle with sharp swords and cut deeply into each other's philosophy. Let the voters see the wounds and clearly understand the weak points in their arguments."

In the months that followed, the two campaigns did all they could to oblige the <u>Durham Morning Herald</u>!

The 1984 Helms campaign focused on three themes.

Theme One: The Governor had a well-established track record of straddling the fence on issues to avoid antagonizing any portion of the electorate. One cartoon in a liberal newspaper lampooned Hunts' habit of standing on both sides of issues this way: "Some of my friends are for it; some of friends are against it. I stand with my friends."

The Helms campaign exploited Hunt's wishy-washy stands by running a series of TV and radio ads with the tag line "Where do you stand, Jim?"

Theme Two: Jim Hunt's support of Walter Mondale was also an issue in the campaign. Hunt headed up a Democratic Presidential Rules Commission that wrote rules favorable to Mondale's candidacy. In December of 1983, the Wilmington (N.C.) Morning Star noted Hunt's role in delivering the nomination to Mondale by saying, "the success of the Hunt Commission is evident in the grip Mondale has on the nomination at this point." (December 26, 1983) Hunt had also been close to the Carter-Mondale Administration. Helms' TV ads repeatedly referred to "Jim Hunt — a Mondale liberal."

Hunt, with the help of his liberal allies in the news media, tried to distance himself from Mondale. After Hunt tried to disassociate himself from the Mondale-liberal camp, Helms remarked that he is a "Mondale-liberal and ashamed of it; I'm a Reagan conservative and proud of it."

Charlotte Observer editor and frantic liberal Richard Oppel wrote a column defending Hunt, saying: "I get tired of Helms saying *I'm a Reagan conservative, Hunt is a Mondale liberal...'* Hunt certainly is to the left of Helms but does anyone truly believe he is politically close to Mondale?"

Well yes. Two people as a matter of fact: One of Jim Hunt's top political gurus *and* Jim Hunt himself. Hunt operative Joe Pell told the <u>Raleigh News and Observer</u> on February 18, 1982 that "He [Hunt] is closer to Mondale than any of the names I have seen mentioned for 1984."

And on February 13, 1982, Jim Hunt himself signed a fundraising letter for Mondale's political action committee in which Hunt declared: "He (Mondale) has served us well during his many years in the United States Senate... you know his potential for leadership in our nation in the future... Walter Mondale believes as you and I do in the very best for the Democratic Party." This kind of deception was typical of the liberal editors in North Carolina.

Some moderate-to-conservative Democrats in Eastern North Carolina warned Hunt and the state Democratic Party machinery (which Hunt controlled) that the embrace of liberal politicians could be fatal in the November elections.

On August 23, 1982, the <u>Washington (N.C.) Daily News</u> — a Democratic newspaper — ran this editorial,
"It Is Our Fault."

"After November elections, particularly in presidential election years, here in North Carolina many of us who are Democrats take political inventory of what has happened, and sometimes we have to ask "why."

We cannot say that Republicans will or will not renominate Ronald Reagan in 1984. But we can come very near saying right now that the road our Democratic leadership in N.C. continues to travel, it makes little difference whom the Republicans nominate.

The list of far out liberal Democrats seems to be the only list our leadership ever looks at. We have picked a McGovern type Democrat, Senator Alan Cranston of California, to deliver our Jackson-Jefferson Day address next time. He is as liberal as they come, and we cannot even begin to get Democrats back in there when all we have to offer them are liberals of his vintage.

As Democrats, we bemoan the fact that so many registered Democrats vote for Jesse Helms. And this editor is among the moaners.

But in truth we, as Democrats, are getting what we ask for when we continue to invite only liberals to come to our state for important party addresses."

That warning would prove prophetic.

Theme Three: Jim Hunt's support of tax increases. In 1984, the National Governor's Conference passed a resolution calling for a tax increase of over $200 billion to balance the budget. Jim Hunt voted for the resolution.

The Helms campaign put out a press release criticizing Hunt's vote for the tax increase. The next morning, when Helms campaign staffers arrived at their Raleigh offices and opened up their <u>Raleigh News and Observer</u> newspapers, they could not believe their eyes. The February 29, 1984 headline in the <u>News and Observer</u> blared: "Hunt votes for plan to increase taxes, prompting quick criticism from Helms."

It was going to be hard for Hunt to disavow his vote for the tax increase after the most pro-Hunt, anti-Helms newspaper in the country printed that headline.

The Helms news release went out late in the day, and some Helms staffers wondered if virulently anti-Helms <u>News and Observer</u> editor Claude Sitton had left for the day when the story was filed. It seemed inconceivable that he would have allowed that headline to be printed in his newspaper.

At least 16 other newspapers followed with stories about Hunt voting for the big tax increase. Even worse, the Helms campaign was able to obtain videotape of Hunt raising his hand in favor of the tax increase.

Hunt's vote for the tax increase, his flip-flops on issues and his ties to unpopular presidential candidate Walter Mondale ultimately sank his quest for the Senate.

But Hunt did not go down without a fight. He launched a brutal TV advertising campaign against Helms. Hunt sought to portray Helms as too "right-wing" for North Carolina and more concerned about foreign policy than North Carolina interests.

Perhaps Hunt's most memorable ad was the so-called "Dead Bodies" TV spot. Gunshots are heard, dead bodies in El Salvador are littered on the screen. The Hunt announcer seeks to blame Helms for the deaths. Many North Carolinians thought the "Dead Bodies" ad went too far. Voters were not prepared to believe that Helms (or Hunt) would sanction murder.

The two candidates also engaged in four grueling debates which were televised statewide. On November 6, 1984 Helms' message prevailed in the biggest Senate race in U.S. history.

1990 Helms vs. Gantt I
Harvey Gantt Falls Due to "Blight on his Record"

In 1990, Senator Helms faced former Charlotte Mayor Harvey Gantt. The race turned out to be surprisingly close, until the end when the Helms campaign brought Gantt's "Achilles heel" to the attention of North Carolina voters.

The media has a simplistic explanation for Jesse Helms' 1990 triumph over Harvey Gantt. They claim that a Helms campaign ad exposing Harvey Gantt's support for affirmative action defeated Gantt. In reality the ad only ran for a few days — <u>not</u> enough to change the outcome of the race. The real knockout punch was delivered by the television ad documenting Gantt's shady television license deal.

In 1984-1987, Harvey Gantt had engaged in a dubious deal to use his minority status to acquire a TV station license from the FEC — and then immediately sell it to a white-owned corporation for a huge profit. The shady transaction was roundly criticized by liberal newspapers like the <u>Raleigh News and Observer</u> and the <u>Charlotte Observer</u>.

A March 26, 1986 <u>Charlotte Observer</u> editorial stated "Mr. Gantt and his colleagues took advantage of the FEC's interest in helping minorities get into the television business and now plan to take a quick and very large profit by getting out of the television business."

A Charlotte civil rights group claimed Gantt obtained the TV station license "under false pretense." (<u>Charlotte Observer</u>, October 29, 1987)

A spokesman for People United for Justice, Reverend James Barnett, told the <u>Charlotte Observer</u>: "We feel that the license was granted under special consideration .... because it's a minority group. And if the special consideration was given and now the station is being sold to whites, the question is what does the black community gain .... They were just concerned about lining their pockets." (April 16, 1986)

The 1990 Helms campaign produced a TV spot describing the TV station deal in far more meek terms than Charlotte's civil rights leaders had used.

Nonetheless, the media tried to brand the Helms campaign as "racist" for daring to criticize (in milder terms) the same shady TV station deal that others had previously denounced. This ad, which revealed a character flaw in Gantt, was the fatal blow of the 1990 campaign.

Then there was Senator Helms' famous "Hands" TV ad. Virtually every liberal political pundit in America described as "racist" this 1990 Helms campaign ad exposing Harvey Gantt's support of a Civil Rights bill that was actually a racial quotas bill.

During the final days of the 1990 campaign, Ted Kennedy tried to push the Senate to override President George Bush's veto of Kennedy's racial quotas bill. (The United States Chamber of Commerce referenced the quota aspect of the bill on June 18, 1990 by stating: "Employers will impose a quota system and require that hiring decisions be based on race.") Helms voted against Kennedy's quota bill, and the override attempt failed by one vote.

An October 25, 1990 Charlotte Observer article headlined "Gantt Seizes on Veto in UNCC Speech," makes clear that it was Gantt who injected the racial quotas bill into the campaign. The Charlotte Observer quotes Gantt saying: "That just goes to show if Harvey Gantt was in the Senate today, it [the vote on the quota bill] would have gone a different way."

The Helms campaign responded with a TV ad that described Gantt's position in straightforward terms. As a white male crumbles a rejection letter, the announcer states: "You needed that job and you were the most qualified. But they had to give it to a minority because of a racial quota."

Liberal editors and politicians were outraged. "Racism" they cried. The national media repeatedly refused to acknowledge that it was Harvey Gantt who injected the racial quotas bill into the campaign in the first place. It seems that the media believed that Gantt was free to criticize Helms for opposing the quota bill, but Helms should not be allowed to respond.

Douglas Bailey, a Republican political consultant in Washington (not affiliated with the Helms campaign), looked at the use of the man's hands in the ad from a logical, television-savvy perspective: "Television is a visual medium and often an emotional one. If you take away the image of the man's hands crumpling the paper in the Jesse Helms ad, you wind up with what? A pretty dry discussion of racial quotas. You need to grab a voter's attention and hold it, and the chances are the voter is sitting there with a remote control, switching channels." (<u>Chicago Tribune</u>, November 19, 1990)

The <u>Chicago Tribune</u> itself went even further, noting that "the impact of television, generally conceded after 40 years to be the most powerful influence in American culture, is not understood, even — <u>or perhaps especially</u> — by its noisiest critics." (November 19, 1990)

During the final weeks of the 1990 campaign, Gantt's media strategist Mandy Grunwald told the <u>New York Times</u>: "His [Helms'] campaigns are more competent than 99% of the campaigns in the country."

That was a fact that media liberals could not bear to acknowledge in 1990, after Senator Jesse Helms won his fourth race.

The media has also never wished to acknowledge the extent to which Gantt has used the "racist" epithet to malign a wide variety of political opponents:

1987 In a speech in Florida, Gantt accused Ronald Reagan's Administration of fostering a new era of racism.

1991 Gantt smeared the entire Republican Party as racist in a national fundraising letter for the Democratic Party. In an August 15, 1991 article headlined "Gantt Charges GOP Playing Racial Politics," the <u>Charlotte Observer</u> notes that Gantt claims: "The Republicans have stepped up their efforts to turn white Americans against African-Americans."

1992   Harvey Gantt even made the incredible assertion that any politician who talks about "traditional values" is really a racist. The <u>Charlotte Observer</u>, in an April article headlined "**Racism a 'traditional value,' Gantt says**" reported that "Harvey Gantt, speaking at the Orange County Democratic convention last weekend said politicians who preach a return to traditional values are making veiled appeals to racism, sexism and other forms of bigotry."

1996   When Democratic businessman Charles Sanders dared to run against Gantt in the 1996 Democratic primary for the U.S. Senate, Gantt smeared him for — you guessed it — running a racist campaign. The headline in the <u>Fayetteville (N.C.) Observer-Times</u> on April 23, 1996 was revealing: "Gantt says Sanders playing race card." Gantt told another newspaper that "the cynical thing is that he [Sanders] is saying is that he can beat Jesse Helms because he is white." (<u>Charlotte Post</u>, April 18, 1996)

Of course, Sanders never said that.

Even some black supporters of Harvey Gantt acknowledged that Gantt's cries of racism had gone too far. The <u>Charlotte Post</u> quoted Julius Chambers, the chancellor of North Carolina Central University — and a Gantt supporter — as saying: "I would doubt whether Charlie Sanders was injecting race into the campaign. I have never seen Charlie do anything racist."

Charlie Sanders. Ronald Reagan. The Republican Party. People who believe in traditional values. Jesse Helms. Gantt and his liberal allies have maligned all of them as racist.

And in a complete abdication of their professional responsibilities, the national media (and to a lesser extent, the North Carolina media) have steadfastly refused to report about Gantt's *consistent pattern* of vilifying all his opponents as "racist."

They also failed to hold Gantt accountable for other statements he made on the issue of race. Gantt, a former mayor of Charlotte, made this incredibly explosive statement: "A mayor is not worth his salt if he cannot help create a few black millionaires by the time his term is over." St. Petersburg Times, January 17, 1987) The media conveniently ignored Gantt's racially-tinged pronouncement.

1996 Helms vs. Gantt II

Jesse Helms and Harvey Gantt faced off for a second time in 1996. Unlike in 1990, the Helms campaign took control of the agenda from the outset. In between 1990 and 1996, Gantt had spoken to the ACLU, endorsed a "gay rights" resolution in Charlotte and openly admitted that he was a liberal. The Helms campaign prepared a television spot recounting Gantt's promotion of the liberal agenda from 1990 to 1996. Internal Helms polling produced a clear and simple outline of what needed to be done to win. If the Helms campaign succeeded in bringing Gantt's liberal record to the voters *before* Gantt had a chance to redefine himself as a moderate (in other words, run away from his record), Helms would win. If Gantt were allowed to "move back to the center," the race would be much tighter.

The first Helms television spot was lethal — exposing Gantt as a liberal. Subsequent ads on taxes, welfare reform and gay rights reinforced the liberal theme.

Gantt's top advisor, Jim Andrews, did a credible job of running a disciplined campaign, stressing "kitchen table" issues. But his candidate's promotion of liberal causes during "the off-season" between 1990 and 1996 made it impossible for the campaign to effectively reposition Gantt in the center.

In 1996, Jesse Helms won his fifth and final race for the Senate, with 53% of the vote.

After the campaign, Gantt strategist Jim Andrews said: "We think we ran as good and as aggressive a campaign as we could run against him. We ran a disciplined race, and it did not work. There's something special and different about Helms." (Raleigh News and Observer, November 7, 1996)

Andrews went on to note that race did not have nearly as much impact on the campaign as some in the media thought: "Does race have an impact? Not as much as you think." (Raleigh News and Observer, November 7, 1996)

After Jesse Helms had won his fifth race, Bill Snider, former editor of the Greensboro News and Record, summed up Helms' electoral success:

"I think he has become the most popular politician that North Carolina has produced, even beyond Jim Hunt, who couldn't quite make the grade against him in 1984 .... He could probably hold the office as long as he cares to." (<u>Raleigh News and Observer</u>, November 7, 1996)

And The World Came His Way

Conclusion

Some in the media have made a career out of portraying Senator Jesse Helms as a man wistfully looking backwards toward the past. Spiteful cartoonists — who resent Senator Helms' enormous power — often portray him in a Neanderthal outfit with a club. There is no question that Jesse Helms longs for a return to certain fundamental values like "helping pull the wagon instead of riding in it" as he said in a 1996 TV commercial. Jesse Helms believes that certain simple truths are valid now and forever. You should not spend more than you take in, that the individual, not the government, is entitled to the fruit of his labor, and that socialism, in all its forms, cannot produce economic success for the masses in any civilization — here or abroad.

Jesse Helms believes in the simple philosophy of peace through strength.

But the media's caricature of Jesse Helms as a man continually looking backwards is woefully inaccurate.

Jesse Helms has been so far ahead on so many issues that many in the media simply cannot remember that far back.

The first legislation Senator Helms introduced when he arrived in the U.S. Senate was the Balanced Budget Amendment. He has been a persistent advocate of reigning in runaway government spending. Senator Helms warned of the consequences of excessive big government spending long before Ronald Reagan arrived in Washington. He was pilloried by <u>The Raleigh News and Observer</u> as "Senator No" for his opposition to big government welfare programs.

By the time the 1980s rolled around, the destructive deficits that Helms had warned about were clear for all to see (even clear to people who live in the fog of Washington D.C.). By the 1990s, Senators, Congressmen, moderate Republican Governors, and even Bill Clinton were singing the praises of something they called "welfare reform." This "newly discovered" welfare reform called for people to find work instead of relying on welfare. The entire political landscape had come Helms' way. It seems everyone now wanted to be known as "Senator No" when it came to the issue of out-of-control government spending.

Senator Jesse Helms was also one of the earliest proponents of the flat tax.

On the twin pillars of economic policy for taxes and government spending — Senator Jesse Helms has been in the forefront. He was advocating less government spending and a reformed tax code over a decade before these two positions became accepted Republican doctrine.

Senator Jesse Helms' leadership has been felt even more strongly in the area of foreign policy and national defense.

It was Senator Jesse Helms who sounded the alarm in 1979 against allowing a terrorist base to be established in Nicaragua — a terrorist base that was being constructed with the active assistance of the Iranians, the Iraqis, the Libyans, the Algerians and other terrorist sponsoring states.

Twenty-two years later, in 2001, a very courageous President George W. Bush ushered in the so-called "Bush doctrine: the U.S. shall not allow any state to harbor terrorists that threaten the United States."

From 1979-1990, Senator Jesse Helms had led the same crusade against allowing Nicaragua to establish a terrorist base less than a three-hour plane trip from our soil. He was persistent, dogmatic and yes, uncompromising in insisting that the U.S. must arm the Contras. As with the Northern Alliance in Afghanistan, who were written off as a "rag-tag bunch of untrained, undisciplined soldiers who are involved in gross misconduct, involved in the drug trade and have absolutely no chance of dislodging the established central government," the media attacked the Contras, who were America's allies in the War on Terrorism in Nicaragua in the 1980s.

The obvious difference: the attack on the World Trade Center made it much easier to attract public backing for American aid to the Northern Alliance. After September 11, 2001, this country was determined to use whomever and whatever it took to get Al Qaeda and the Taliban.

During the 1980s, it was not that easy to attract public support — and elected officials' support — for fighting the establishment of a terrorist regime in Nicaragua. In the 1980s it was "les bontemp rollez" in the United States, and very few people wanted to upset the apple cart by fighting a war in the backwoods of Central America.

The cause was right, but the public support was not there. It takes a very special leader to rise up and say we must fight a war anyway. During the 1980s, Jesse Helms was that man.

Fortunately, he understood, many years before his countrymen did, the threat posed by allowing terrorists to go unchallenged.

And he successfully led the charge to expel the terrorists from Central America.

Senator Jesse Helms was speaking out about the Mexican drug trade long before the death of DEA agent Enrique S. Camarena on February 9, 1985 and the subsequent movie about his life.

Senator Helms was warning about the dangers posed by Iraqi dictator Saddam Hussein years before the Gulf War.

During the 1980s Jesse Helms cautioned against relying on Communist China as a partner. After China stole our military secrets and attempted to buy our elections in the 1990s, officials in Washington began to wake up to the threat posed by an aggressive China.

As he leaves office, Senator Helms' judgment and leadership on issues has been validated by history on issue after issue.

The world has, indeed, come Helms' way.

His critics' chief remaining complaints are that he "was too rigid," he "doesn't compromise" and "he doesn't go along with the rest of the crowd in Washington."

In reality, Senator Helms has compromised on dollars and cents matters on numerous occasions — for example, when the Reagan Administration needed his help on key votes.

But on matters of principle, Senator Helms was everything his critics said he was — "unyielding," "rigid," and "uncompromising."

Given the benefit of history — the collapse of the Soviet empire and the Middle Eastern terrorist threat to our nation — on which major principles would his detractors have had him compromise?

In 1976, virtually everyone else in Congress had coalesced around Gerald Ford and against Ronald Reagan. The Reagan campaign began negotiating with Ford's team to get Reagan out of the race. It would have been a humiliating exit that would have ended Ronald Reagan's career in 1976. But Helms would not go along to get along. He encouraged Reagan to come to North Carolina and fight on. Helms and his political operatives blanketed North Carolina with the message that Gerald Ford was giving away the Panama Canal. Reagan won a stunning victory in North Carolina and went on the challenge Ford all the way to the convention. Reagan emerged stronger than ever and won the presidency in 1980.

Had Jesse Helms "gone along with everyone else in Washington" in 1976, there would have been no Reagan presidency. There would have been no Reagan landslide of 1980 that produced a Republican Senate. There would have been no Reagan-led defeat of the Soviet empire and the resulting freedom for hundreds of millions of people behind the "Iron Curtain."

Given the events of September 11, 2001, do his detractors wish he had "compromised" on Nicaragua and allowed the establishment of a terrorist base for the Libyans, Iraqis, Iranians and other militants to use to strike the U.S.?

There were numerous times when key players in the State Department and the White House wanted to cut a deal or compromise to "put the Contra issue behind them." Some in the State Department were growing weary of the issue because our European allies were opposed to our policy. Some in the White House wanted the issue to go away for purely political reasons. The issue was not popular with voters, particularly swing voters who are critical in close elections. But Helms felt a commitment to something more important than swing voters in the next election. He knew what was at stake. And every time a plan came up to abandon the Contras, Helms, in effect, said "over my dead body." He publicly challenged those in the Administration who he did not feel were faithful to the President's agenda in Central America. There would be no compromise from Jesse Helms on the establishment of a terrorist beachhead in Central America.

With 20/20 hindsight, most Americans are thankful that there was one man of principle, one man who would not compromise, one man who would not go along with a back-door deal when the security of his country was at stake.

That is the legacy of Jesse A. Helms.

How you can help

The Jesse Helms Center relies on friends and concerned Americans like you to help us continue to preserve and promote the principles of traditional values, representative democracy and free enterprise upon which U.S. Senator Jesse Helms has built his life and career. Printing and distribution of this book is paid for from voluntary donations. I urge you to consider a donation to help the work of the Jesse Helms Center to continue. And I also urge you to order more books to distribute to friends and family who are interested in preserving and promoting the values and principles espoused by Senator Jesse Helms.

Books are $8.95 each. Please add $2.00 postage & handling per book ordered. Send your book orders and donations to:

The Jesse Helms Center
P.O. Box 247
Wingate, N.C. 28174

Or visit our website at: www.jessehelmscenter.org

And The World Came His Way